EFT
EMOTIONAL FREEDOM TECHNIQUES

GET CERTIFIED IN EFT!

EFT certification is a rewarding experience. It opens up new career horizons, as well as personal healing opportunities.

You can obtain CE/CME credits if you're a physician (American Medical Association), nurse (American Nurses Credentialing Commission), psychologist (American Psychological Association) or social worker (NASWB) for Clinical EFT training, which provides a step-by-step process for mastering the "evidence-based" form of EFT.

To enroll click "Certification" at www.EFTUniverse.com

EFT
EMOTIONAL FREEDOM TECHNIQUES
EFTUniverse.com

FOR YOUR PROFESSIONAL BOOKSHELF

from

ENERGY PSYCHOLOGY PRESS

The Human Hologram
Living Your Life in Harmony with the Unified Field
By Dr. Robin Kelly

A London-trained physician presents evidence that our physical bodies are perpetually being formed upon an invisible field of information, and that as our consciousness interacts with that field, we can optimize our health.

Softcover, 6" x 9", 256 pages $16.95

Soul Medicine
Awakening Your Inner Blueprint for Abundant Health and Energy
By Norman Shealy, MD, PhD, and Dawson Church, PhD

A neurosurgeon and founder of the American Holistic Medical Association, Shealy teams up with health researcher Dawson Church to present the latest studies showing the healing effects of energy, intention and consciousness.

Softcover, 6" x 9", 296 pages $17.95

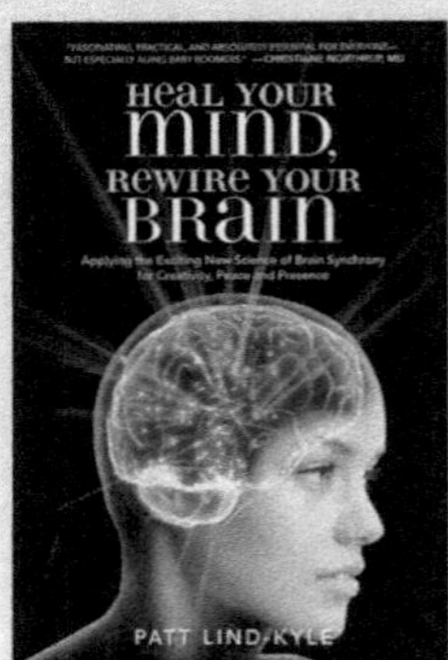

Heal Your Mind, Rewire Your Brain
Applying the Exciting New Science of Brain Plasticity for Creativity, Peace and Presence
By Patt Lind-Kyle, MA

Applies the latest exciting scientific discoveries in a practical, step-by-step program that literally rewires neural connections in the brain for greater happiness.

Hardcover, 6" x 9", 32 Illustrations, 253 pages $26.95

Creating Healing Relationships
Professional Standards for Energy Therapy Practitioners
By Dorothea Hover-Kramer, EdD, RN, DCEP

Written by the co-founder of ACEP, the professional organization for Energy Psychology, this is the first book to seriously address the need for professional standards in the rapidly growing field of energy healing.

Hardcover, 6" x 9", 256 pages $35

Body Eloquence
The Power of Myth and Story to Awaken the Body's Energies
By Nancy Mellon, MFT with Ashley Ramsden

Have you ever had an ache or pain, and wished your body could talk to you and tell you what was wrong? Drawing from mythology, medicine, biology and energetic healing, this book shows the messages that our organs are communicating to us.

Trade Paper, 7" x 10", 15 Illustrations, 260 pages $18.95

Energy Healer's Ethics Handbook
By David Feinstein, PhD, with Donna Eden

This comprehensive, case-oriented guide allows veterans of the field and newcomers alike to work through a wide range of ethical dilemmas before they arise, helping you to prevent professional errors that could hurt you, your clients, and your practice.

Hardcover, 6" x 9", 210 pages $39

ENERGY PSYCHOLOGY PRESS

Order now at EnergyPsychologyPress.com

Energy Psychology
Theory, Research, and Treatment

A Journal of the National Institute for Integrative Healthcare (NIIH.org)

www.EnergyPsychologyJournal.org

Energy Psychology: Theory, Research, and Treatment is a peer-reviewed professional journal dedicated to reporting developments in the field of energy psychology (EP) that are of interest to health care professionals and researchers. It contains original empirical research into the efficacy of EP methods; theoretical, experimental, and basic science papers illuminating the mechanisms of action of EP; clinical insights on the application of EP to various populations, and interfaces with other interventions; book reviews, and abstracts published in other journals that are of relevance to the EP field. Its goal is to further the development of EP as an evidence-based method in the healing sciences. It conforms to the editorial, stylistic, and ethical standards of the American Psychological Association (APA.org).

Energy Psychology: Theory, Research, and Treatment (ISSN 1949-6575) is published biannually (November and May) by Energy Psychology Press, PO Box 442, Fulton, CA 95439. For customer service or advertising information, contact 707-237-6951 or energypsychologypress@gmail.com.

POSTMASTER: Send address changes to: *Energy Psychology* journal, PO Box 442, Fulton, CA 95439.

YEARLY SUBSCRIPTION RATES: $49.95 per issue, $99.95 per year.

AUTHOR ENQUIRIES: Submit paper copies of proposed papers to *Energy Psychology* journal, PO Box 442, Fulton, CA 95439. Include an e-mail address and phone number for the corresponding author. All submissions should conform fully to the requirements of the *Publication Manual of the American Psychological Association,* sixth edition. Include a cover letter as specified on the "Submissions" link at www.EnergyPsychologyJournal.org, and manuscripts should be prepared in conformity with the other standards published there. Acceptance or rejection will be made via e-mail; paper copies will not be returned. If a submission is accepted for peer review, all subsequent contact will occur via e-mail. Deadline for Spring issue submissions is Jan 15 of each year, and July 15 for Fall issue.

REPRINTS: Back issues are available for $49.95. Reprint ordering information may be found at www.EnergyPsychologyPress.com. To order 100 or more copies of a particular paper, contact energypsychologypress@gmail.com.

Contents

May 2022 • Volume 14, Number 1

About

ENERGY PSYCHOLOGY: THEORY, RESEARCH, AND TREATMENT

Energy Psychology (EP) is an evolving and maturing field that is rapidly meeting the standards of proof for "evidence-based" practice. Studies of EP have demonstrated its efficacy for a wide range of psychological and physical problems, from phobias to pain to posttraumatic stress disorder. EP is now being researched in hospital systems such as Britain's National Health Service (NHS), large private hospital chains such as Kaiser Permanente and Sutter Health, and the United States Department of Veterans Affairs (VA). By providing a rigorous, high-quality, peer-reviewed platform for the publication of research results, theory, and clinical insights, this journal provides a forum for the exchange of the key discoveries and ideas that drive the EP field forward.

—Dawson Church, PhD
Editor, *Energy Psychology: Theory, Research, and Treatment*

The journal publishes work in the following areas:

EDITORIAL ESSAYS include guest editorials from some of the best thinkers and researchers in EP today;

ORIGINAL RESEARCH provides empirical evidence for various EP methods;

CLINICAL REPORTS describe the use of EP with challenging conditions and specific populations and provide guidance for empirical research;

INTERFACES WITH OTHER THERAPIES show how EP is typically used in conjunction with other methods, such as cognitive behavior therapy (CBT), mindfulness therapy, addiction counseling, sports psychology, medicine, energy medicine, meditation, and life coaching;

REVIEW ARTICLES are theoretical papers, literature reviews, reports of innovations, and analyses that explore issues from the professional condition of EP to the physiological mechanisms of action of EP;

BOOK REVIEWS cover new and classic EP-related titles;

ABSTRACTS published in other journals relevant to EP are reprinted.

EDITORIAL BOARD

The Whole World Smiles with You

Dawson Church

"When you're smiling, when you're smiling, the whole world smiles with you." Thus crooned Frank Sinatra in his 1950 album *Swing and Dance.*

Research is now showing that Sinatra was teaching science as well as making music. A paper published in the journal *Trends in Cognitive Sciences* reviews the evidence for the contagious power of smiling (Wood et al., 2016).

It shows that human beings extract emotional meaning from the facial expressions of others. We then unconsciously mimic them. This can result in us feeling emotions similar to those we are observing. For instance, if you're interacting with a team member whose facial expression your brain interprets as "sad," you might unconsciously draw your face into a similar expression. This helps you recognize the other's emotion by associating it with times in your past when you had similar experiences.

Paula Niedenthal, one of the study authors, adds these insights: "You reflect on your emotional feelings and then you generate some sort of recognition judgment, and the most important thing that results is that you take the appropriate action—you approach the person or you avoid the person. Your own emotional reaction to the face changes your perception of how you see the face, in such a way that provides you more information about what it means."

This presents a barrier to people who have impaired ability to recognize emotions, such as those with autism, cognitive impairment, or facial paralysis. Niedenthal notes, "There are some symptoms in autism where lack of facial mimicry may in part be due to suppression of eye contact... it may be overstimulating socially to engage in eye contact, but under certain conditions, if you encourage eye contact, the benefit is spontaneous or automatic facial mimicry."

The process occurs so quickly that it's below the processing threshold of the conscious mind. The brain identifies the meaning behind another person's smile or frown in a few milliseconds.

We're doing this automatically all the time. This can produce a phenomenon called "emotional contagion." In my book *Mind to Matter*, I provide many examples of how emotions can spread with astonishing speed. Within a few days, your smile might affect hundreds of thousands of other people.

Realizing that we're producing emotional contagion allows us to take conscious control of the process. You can smile deliberately.

Smiling can even make the difference between life and death. A man we'll call "Jim" tells the following story.

"I was going through one of the low points in my life. My wife Maddy had recently left me, taking the kids with her. I missed them so bad I felt this gnawing ache in my gut every day.

"Then the recession hit and I lost my job. For several months I applied for position after position and got turned down every time. I began to feel worthless. I contemplated suicide on and off. Then one day I decided to do it. Life just didn't seem worth living anymore.

"I parked at the Golden Gate Bridge lot. My plan was to walk across to the middle and jump off the railing.

"At the pedestrian crossing to the bridge, the light turned red just as I got there. I stopped and waited, as did all the cars going in my direction. I looked at the car next to me. In it sat a peaceful looking woman with long gray hair. She turned and looked at me. She looked deep into my eyes.

"Then her face broke into the biggest smile you can imagine. I felt love simply radiating out from her. It reached down and warmed the center of my soul.

"I suddenly felt as though everything was going to be okay. I turned around and took a walk around the Presidio Park. I heard the birds singing. I noticed the flowers blooming. I saw the reflection of the trees in the pond and I knew everything was going to turn out fine. And it did.

"That woman's smile changed my life."

Once we understand the power of emotional contagion, we can begin to use it for positive effect. When you see your children or spouse in the morning, smile! If you're on a video call, smile at every person in the virtual room. In a live audience, smile. As you're walking through the shopping mall, smile at the people you see. You will be surprised at how often they smile back.

Even when I'm sitting at my computer answering emails, I smile at the invisible people with whom I'm corresponding. I'm smiling right now as I write this essay for you.

So smile long and often! And notice how the whole world smiles with you.

References

Church, D. (2018). *Mind to matter: The astonishing science of how your brain creates material reality.* Carlsbad, CA: Hay House.

Wood, A., Rychlowska, M., Korb, S., & Niedenthal, P. (2016). Fashioning the face: sensorimotor simulation contributes to facial expression recognition. *Trends in Cognitive Sciences, 20*(3), 227–240.

ORIGINAL RESEARCH

Therapists' Observations in Reduction of Unpleasant Emotions Following Advanced Integrative Therapy Interventions

Gregory P. Brown, Kavita Batra, Suzie S. Hong, Robert Sottile, Raveena Bakhru, and Emily Dorin

All affiliated with Kirk Kerkorian School of Medicine at University of Nevada Las Vegas, USA

Abstract

Objective: To assess the potential clinical efficacy of a novel model of energy psychology intervention, Advanced Integrative Therapy (AIT), this pilot study assessed clinician perceptions of AIT through a cross-sectional survey. **Methods:** A 17-item web-based questionnaire was administered to AIT therapists in November of 2021. The survey included clinician demographics and the clinician-observed response to AIT treatment based upon changes in reported Subjective Units of Distress (SUD), the associated emotion, and somatic sensation (when present). **Results:** A total of 76 complete responses were analyzed. The sample respondents were predominantly female (81.6%) and non-Hispanic white (68%). Over 80% of the respondents reported using AIT with their clients within the past six months and a significant proportion of participants self-assessed their AIT skills as of proficient or expert level. As reported by the therapists, 77% of the sessions described were used to clear patterns of negative events rather than a single event. Over 75% of events were identified as being either since childhood or otherwise chronic in nature. The average pre-AIT intervention SUD score was reported as 8.3±2.7 out of 10, which in 92% of cases, dropped to either 0 or 1 following a single session of AIT. **Conclusions:** Although this pilot study was limited to clinician responses in assessment of the ability of AIT to reduce the negative emotions related to past traumatic events, the initial observations were supportive of the potential clinical utility of this energy psychology technique. The findings suggest that additional client-based assessments and randomized clinical trials with known therapies as a control are warranted to continue the systematic observation of AIT.

Keywords: energy psychology, Advanced Integrative Therapy, Emotional Freedom Technique, Thought Field Therapy

Gregory P. Brown, MD, is professor of psychiatry and director of the psychiatry residency training. **Kavita Batra, PhD,** is an assistant professor and medical research biostatistician. **Suzie S. Hong, DO,** is a second-year psychiatry resident. **Robert Sottile** is a medical student. **Raveena Bakhru, DO,** and **Emily Dorin, DO,** are first-year psychiatry residents. **Correspondence:** Gregory P. Brown, MD, Department of Psychiatry and Behavioral Health, Kirk Kerkorian School of Medicine, University of Nevada Las Vegas, 3014 West Charleston Blvd., Suite 130, Las Vegas, NV 89102, USA; email: gregory.brown1@unlv.edu. **Disclosure:** The authors declare no conflicts of interest.

Energy psychology utilizes aspects of a diverse set of therapeutic interventions combining Western treatment modalities, such as exposure therapy and cognitive behavior therapy (CBT), with Eastern somatic techniques (König et al., 2019). The study and use of energy-based psychotherapies began more than 40 years ago, when in the early 1980s, Roger Callahan introduced a novel treatment for specific phobias known as Thought Field Therapy (TFT).

This intervention uses a unique algorithm to select a treatment that incorporates the stimulation of acupressure points to process troublesome thoughts (Callahan, 2001; Clond, 2016). The protocol for Emotional Freedom Techniques (EFT), published by Craig and Fowlie in 1995, described a simplified adaptation of TFT that used verbal reframing of a traumatic thought combined with guided acupressure-point (acupoint) tapping (Church et al., 2020; Clond, 2016).

Virtually all energy psychology–based techniques include access to a memory from an earlier traumatic event, a verbal phrase or component, and a tactile component, the combination of which appears to reduce the affect associated with the troublesome memory or trauma (Church et al., 2020; Clond, 2016; Dincer & Inangil, 2021). It is thought that the somatic components deployed in EFT and other energy psychology treatments act similarly to acupuncture by reducing limbic system activation, thereby blunting the hyperactive sympathetic stress response that is coupled to the traumatic memory of interest (Church et al., 2020; Clond, 2016; Dincer & Inangil, 2021; Feinstein, 2021). Electroencephalogram (EEG) and functional magnetic resonance imaging (fMRI) studies suggest that the combination of tapping with the repeated reminder phrase creates new neural pathways that produce durable results (Engebretson & Wardell, 2007; König et al., 2019). Further, additional research comparing tapping on sham points and tapping on acupressure points suggests that the somatic component of energy psychology treatment is essential (Church et al., 2020). Other theoretical explanations include memory reconsolidation theory (Lee et al., 2017), split attention models, and polyvagal theory of trauma (Craik et al., 1996; Kolacz et al., 2019; Morris et al., 2014).

In 2021, a review of 245 energy psychology studies suggested six common features shared by these hybridized techniques (Feinstein, 2021). Importantly, the author noted that therapies such as EFT offered significant symptom improvements for multiple disorders that were similar in effect size (efficacy) and at least as durable as the effects of traditional "gold standard" therapies, such as CBT. Energy-based therapies have been broadly deployed since their introduction in the 1980s, and they have been used to treat a wide range of psychiatric disorders including depression in post-menopausal women, PTSD, test anxiety, substance abuse, specific phobias, and other anxiety disorders (Bach et al., 2019; Inangil et al., 2020; Khan et al., 2018; Mehdipour et al., 2021). Since 2015, five meta-analyses evaluating the effect size of energy psychology, generally EFT, have been compiled (Church et al., 2020; Clond, 2016; Sebastian & Nelms, 2017). Uniformly, the meta-analyses reported moderate to large effect sizes for energy psychology treatments. In 2017 for instance, Sebastian and Nelms conducted a meta-analysis of seven RCTs evaluating the use of EFT for the treatment of PTSD and reported a large treatment effect size.

EFT and TFT are the best studied and most widely used of the energy psychology techniques, and they are the primary focus of the above cited research. Other methodologies of energy psychology currently in use include, but are not limited to, Tapas Acupressure Technique (TAT), Comprehensive Energy Psychology (CEP), Heart Assisted Therapy (HAT), as well as the subject of this study, Advanced Integrative Therapy (AIT). These techniques have followed a similar developmental timeline but have yet to be the focus of significant empirical research. Each of these modalities includes a specific verbiage and somatic elements of touch or tapping, combined with a form of recall of past traumatic events.

Asha Clinton began developing AIT in 1998 to better integrate certain existing psychotherapies with the somatic/physical techniques used in energy psychology (Advanced Integrative Institute, 2021; American Psychological Association, 2021; Association for Comprehensive Energy Psychology, 2021). In large context, the elements of AIT include three basic interventions: reduction of negative emotional effects of trauma, elimination of negative core beliefs resulting from trauma, and installation of positive belief structures to replace the negative. The AIT definition of the current trauma, termed the Initiating Trauma (Clinton, 2010), consists of an emotion combined with an identified current stressful event. AIT protocol then suggests attempting to discover or identify the first initiating event, termed the Originating Trauma, which is a similar pattern of event and attached emotion from early in life. The "Three Step" process presented in the Basic Course (Clinton, 2010) is designed to clear the emotion from the Initiating Trauma, the Originating Trauma, and the connection between the two (which AIT refers to as the Connecting Trauma). Next, belief structures supporting the negative emotion may then be assessed with the Core Belief Matrices. Core Belief Matrices consist of identified negative beliefs that are associated with the experience of the Originating Trauma. These may be generated spontaneously with the client or reviewed from a list of common limiting beliefs. A subset of limiting beliefs may also be found in the Basic Course Manual (Clinton, 2010). The reduction in the intensity of these beliefs utilizes a similar method as that used on the trauma. The installation of new positive core beliefs has a separate protocol for home use and is often utilized as homework for the patient. There is also a version of AIT for home use referred to as "Quick AIT" (Clinton, 2010).

Unlike EFT, AIT does not utilize tapping of peripheral acupressure points while repeating a "reminder phrase" as its somatic component, but rather incorporates placement of the hand over a series of areas on the body. These regions are traditionally defined as "energy centers" or "chakras," and in the protocols from AIT, hand placement progresses down the midline of the body from the crown of the head to the base of the spine (Advanced Integrative Institute, 2021). The chakra-based energy system theoretically accessed in AIT has been poorly studied relative to the meridian-based/acupressure point system used in modalities such as EFT. A recent review article by Moga (2022, p. 39), however, concludes: "Although there have been few scientific studies of the chakras, evidence suggests that chakras may emit electromagnetic radiation and be associated with underlying nerve plexuses." Moga looked at 16 peer-reviewed articles related to the topic of chakras, including the measurement of frequencies with the use of EMG electrodes, radiofrequency meters, and magnetometers. A comprehensive assessment of the data supporting body energetic systems is beyond the scope of this paper.

Despite the absence of tapping, AIT is a somatic treatment (as described in the Basic Manual, which is available only through taking the Basic AIT Training Course; Clinton, 2010), as the palm of the hand is placed and held on multiple body locations corresponding with the various chakras. Thus, light pressure from the palm of the hand over each bodily location forms the somatic component of the treatment, which is combined with a phrase that is honed to the specific trauma and repeated at each location. There is a pause at each site, where light pressure is maintained to allow for intuitive impressions and insights in addition to a subjective sense of "clearing" of the negative emotion previously associated with the memory. One sequence of this process would be a single "round" of AIT. The phrasing is specific and includes reference to the emotion, the event, and any somatic sensation that arises as part of the memory trace, as described in the Basic Manual (Clinton, 2010).

At present, no randomized controlled trials (RCTs) evaluating the performance of AIT versus other treatment modalities that conforms to the evidentiary standards required by Division 12 of the American Psychological Association (APA) have been conducted. To date, most high-quality studies of energy psychology treatments have focused on a single modality, EFT. Newer variations of energy-based therapies, including AIT, remain poorly studied with little empirical evidence. Despite the limited evidence overall, a recently published detailed case study followed a single client diagnosed with PTSD who was evaluated using serial screening instruments and found to no longer meet the criteria for PTSD after an AIT treatment course of several months (Weaver, 2021).

Recent research suggests that the COVID-19 pandemic has significantly contributed to a global increase in the prevalence of depression, anxiety, and other psychological morbidities (Batra et al., 2020; Batra et al., 2021; Santomauro et al., 2021). As such, the consideration of potentially effective therapies capable of reducing symptoms is of critical importance.

The need for basic research into the potential efficacy of AIT is well-supported by the current lack of relevant literature. Therefore, the purpose of the current retrospective study is to evaluate the reduction of unpleasant emotions as observed by therapists within treatment sessions using AIT interventions as recorded in their own documentation. This was considered a first step in assessing the feasibility of conducting future RCT-level trials.

Methods

Study Design and Sample

This descriptive cross-sectional study involving a single group was conducted in November 2021 using an anonymous web-based survey administered through the Qualtrics platform. Therapists at any level of mental health training and from any country of practice who have used AIT modalities in the past were invited to participate in this survey. The Advanced Integrative Therapy Institute provided an email list of all graduates of any level of training throughout the history of the organization. The investigators of this study used this information to send surveys through the Qualtrics email system. In addition, The Advanced Integrative Therapy Institute provided a separate email invitation to their list through a general link to the survey. The pool of clinicians was international. Clinicians that participated included physicians, psychiatrists, psychologists, licensed social workers, marriage and family therapists, and counselors. Note that being a mental health professional is required to be eligible for AIT training.

Ethical Considerations

An ethical approval regarding the conduct of this research study was obtained from the Institutional Review Board, University of Nevada, Las Vegas, and the project (Protocol ID: UNLV-2021-121) was deemed exempt under the category 2(i) as indicated in Federal regulatory statutes 45CFR46.101(b). Voluntary consent forms and details about the study were attached to the online questionnaire, so participants could make informed choices whether or not to participate. No identifying information was collected regarding the clinician or the client through the course of this protocol.

Questionnaire and Procedure

The survey window was open from November 7, 2021, through November 30, 2021. A 17-item questionnaire was created. The first set of questions focused on clinician demographics and practice (seven items), followed by 10 questions related to the Subjective Units of Distress (SUD) scale pre- and post-intervention, symptom intensity, association of emotion with the initial experience, and changes in bodily sensation related to the initial experience after intervention with Advanced Integrative Therapy. Responses were requested to be based upon chart documentation, although such could not be verified. The time elapsed between treatment and the survey was a survey question and was not formally limited.

The SUD scale was first created by Joseph Wolpe, PhD, in 1969 as a standardized measure of subjective distress (Wolpe, 1973). It has been used as a measure in nearly every tested version of psychotherapy since that time and is considered a validated standardized measure. The SUD rating has been a primary measure of improvement in CBT (Wolpe, 1973). It was used in the assessment of Eye Movement Desensitization and Reprocessing (EMDR) in validating the model experimentally, and it also remains part of the standard protocol for administering EMDR in treatment settings for traumatic experiences. Furthermore, the energy psychology movement has used the scale in efficacy-based studies, as well as in nearly all treatment protocols to measure client perceptions of improvement. The SUD rating has additionally become ubiquitous throughout medical practice. Clinicians often ask what level of anxiety, anger, or depression a patient may be experiencing on a "0-to-10 scale" as a way to measure improvement over time. As per AIT basic protocol, the type of negative emotion and, if present, the bodily sensation attached to the emotion were also included in the question set. The total time to complete the questionnaire was estimated to be less than 10 minutes.

Quality Control and Data Management

Multiple responses from the same participant were prevented by using the "prevent ballot box stuffing" option provided in the Qualtrics. Data files were assessed by the principal investigator and data analyst involved in this project.

Sample Justification

Given the pilot nature of this feasibility study, we used the flat sample size rule of sample size recommendations provided by previous simulation and trial studies. After accounting for the appropriate adjustment factor of 0.5 involving a single group only, the recommended pilot sample size ranged from 30 to 70 subjects, which aligned well with the sample used in this study (Bell et al., 2018; Billingham, et al., 2013; Viechtbauer et al., 2015; Whitehead et al., 2016).

Statistical Analysis

Categorical variables were represented as frequencies and proportions, whereas continuous variables were represented by mean and standard deviations. As this study involved only one group, statistics were limited to the univariate analysis only. The normal approximation to the binomial distribution method was used to calculate 95% confidence intervals of proportions in the univariate analyses. All analyses were conducted using SPSS version 27 (Armonk, NY, USA: IBM Corporation).

Results

A total of 76 complete responses were analyzed. The sample was predominantly female (81.6%) and non-Hispanic white (68%). Clinician responses were from countries all over the world, albeit nearly 46% reported practicing AIT in the United States (Table 1). Over 80% of the respondents reported using AIT with their clients within the past six months, and a significant proportion of the participants self-assessed their AIT skills as of proficient or expert level (Table 1), which is

Table 1. *Demographic Characteristics of Therapists/Respondents Who Have Used Advanced Integrative Therapy (AIT) with Clients (N = 76)*

Variable	Categories/Groups	*n* (%)	95% CI (LCL, UCL)
Age (Mean±SD)	–	53.9±12.6	51.0, 56.8
Gender	Male	10 (13.2)	6.5, 22.8
	Female	62 (81.6)	71.0, 89.5
	Non-binary/Third gender	4 (5.3)	1.5, 12.9
Race/Ethnicity	Non-Hispanic White	52 (68.4)	56.7, 78.6
	Hispanic	15 (19.7)	11.5, 30.5
	Asian	4 (5.3)	1.5, 12.9
	Other, including Black	5 (6.5)	2.2, 14.7
Country of practicing AIT	United States of America	35 (46.1)	34.5, 57.8
	United Kingdom	9 (11.8)	5.5, 21.3
	Canada	3 (3.9)	0.8, 11.1
	France	3 (3.9)	0.8, 11.1
	Germany	3 (3.9)	0.8, 11.1
	Guatemala	7 (9.2)	3.8, 18.1
	Others*	12 (15.7)	8.4, 25.9
	Not reported	4 (5.3)	1.5, 12.9
Used AIT in the past	Recently used within last 6 months	62 (81.6)	71.0, 89.5
	Used over the last 1–3 years	6 (7.9)	3.0, 16.4
	Used over the last 3–5 years	8 (10.5)	4.6,19.7
Trained beyond basic course	Yes	58 (76.3)	65.2, 85.3
	No	13 (17.1)	9.4, 27.4
	Not reported	5 (6.6)	2.2, 14.7
Self-assessment of AIT skills	Basic	4 (5.3)	1.5, 12.9
	Demonstrating	20 (26.3)	16.9, 37.7
	Proficient	40 (52.6)	40.8, 64.2
	Expert	12 (15.8)	8.4, 26.0

Note. All measures are shown as frequency and proportions unless stated otherwise. *Others include China, Argentina, Cayman Islands, Denmark, El Salvador, Spain, Mexico, New Zealand, Poland. SD = Standard deviation; CI = Confidence interval; LCL = Lower Confidence Level; UCL = Upper Confidence Level; Basic = limited in ability or knowledge; Demonstrating = able to perform at a basic level or have some direct experience; Proficient = capable and experienced or able to work independently; Expert = fully capable and experienced or seen as subject matter expert.

Table 2. *Characteristics of Emotions Intervened by Advanced Integrative Therapy (AIT) Sessions as Reported by Therapists/Respondents (N = 76)*

Variable	Categories/Groups	*n* (%)	95% CI (LCL, UCL)
Focus of AIT intervention session	Single event of negative emotions	16 (21.1)	12.5, 31.9
	Pattern of similar events of negative emotions	59 (77.6)	66.6, 86.4
Primary emotion (s) related to event	Anxiety	21 (27.6)	17.9, 39.0
	Fear	12 (15.8)	8.4, 26.0
	Anger	7 (9.2)	3.8, 18.1
	Sadness	13 (17.1)	9.4, 27.5
	Shame	12 (15.8)	8.4, 26.0
	Other emotions including guilt, helplessness, and overwhelm etc.	10 (13.1)	6.5, 22.9
Duration (prior to AIT intervention) of primary emotion which AIT attempted to clear	Since childhood	45 (59.2)	47.3, 70.4
	Chronic emotions which persisted for years	19 (25.0)	15.7, 36.3
	Acute state of emotions which spanned for days, weeks or a few months	11 (14.5)	7.5, 24.4
Location of primary emotion experienced	Head and Neck region	14 (18.4)	10.5, 29.0
	Chest	32 (42.1)	30.9, 54.0
	Abdomen	21 (27.6)	18.0, 39.1
	No physical sensations	7 (9.2)	3.8, 18.1
	Other areas including solar plexus	2 (2.6)	0.3, 9.2

Note. Percentage may not add up to 100% due to some unreported or unknown data by the participants.

congruent with the report that over 75% of participants reported being trained in AIT beyond the first basic course offered (Table 1).

As reported by the therapists, 77% of the sessions described were used to clear patterns of negative events rather than a single event (Table 2). Over 75% of events were identified as being either since childhood or otherwise chronic in nature. The most frequent negative emotions extinguished included anxiety, sadness, and fear followed by other emotions of anger, shame, and helplessness (Table 2). These emotions were most commonly felt in the chest and abdomen in somatic expression (Table 2).

The average pre-AIT intervention SUD score was 8.3±2.7 out of 10, which dropped to either 0 or 1 following a single therapeutic session of AIT in 92% of cases (Table 3). In the vast majority of cases, if a secondary emotion arose, it also cleared within the same session, as did the associated somatic sensations. The average number of rounds of AIT to achieve this improvement within the therapeutic session was three (range 1–6). At follow-up sessions, over 90% of cases reported maintenance of the improvement (Table 3).

Discussion

This pilot study investigated the potential utility of AIT in reducing negative emotions associated with past trauma, based upon the clinical observations of AIT therapists worldwide. Participating therapists observed that past trauma-related negative emotions and the associated somatic sensations could be successfully reduced within a single session of AIT. Furthermore, for a majority of the cases, this observed improvement was maintained in follow-up sessions, indicating a potential lasting benefit beyond the session itself.

A majority of the therapists reported that it was possible in a single session of AIT not only to extinguish emotions related to a single traumatic

Table 3. *Assessment of Advanced Integrative Therapy (AIT) Sessions in Clearing the Emotions of Clients as Reported by Therapists/Respondents (N = 76) Based on the Subjective Units of Distress (SUD) Scale*

Variable	Categories/Groups	*n* (%)	95% CI (LCL, UCL)
Pre AIT-intervention SUD score (Mean±SD)	–	8.3±2.7	
Did SUD score drop to zero or one during AIT session?	Yes	70 (92.1)	83.6, 97.1
	No	6 (7.9)	3.0, 16.4
Was AIT the primary intervention considered to reduce SUD?	Yes	74 (97.4)	90.8, 99.7
	No	2 (2.6)	0.3, 9.2
Average number of rounds needed to clear the emotion	–	3.0±1.0	Min/Max 1–6
After clearing the primary emotion, did the location felt in the physical body change to a new location?	Yes, and that sensation also cleared within the session	27 (35.5)	24.8, 47.3
	Yes, but there was inadequate time to clear the sensation at the second location within the session	16 (21.1)	12.5, 31.9
	No additional location of physical sensation	28 (36.8)	26.1, 48.7
	Not applicable as there was no body location identified for this intervention	5 (6.6)	2.2, 14.7
After clearing primary emotions, did secondary emotion surface?	Yes	59 (77.6)	66.6, 86.4
	No	17 (22.4)	13.6, 33.3
Clearance of secondary emotion	Yes, and the secondary emotion was also cleared within the session	34 (44.7)	33.3, 56.6
	Yes, but there was inadequate time to clear the secondary emotion within that session	25 (32.9)	22.5, 44.6
	No secondary emotions arose	17 (22.4)	13.6, 33.3
Average score of AIT effectiveness reported by therapists (out of 5)	–	4.66±0.64	4.51, 4.81
Follow-up visits	Yes	63 (82.9)	72.5, 90.6
	No (also includes loss to follow-up cases)	13 (17.1)	9.4, 27.5
Persistence in improvement at follow-up sessions*	Yes	58 (92.0)	82.4, 97.3
	No	5 (8.0)	2.6, 17.6

Note. Percentage may not add up to 100% due to some unreported or unknown data. *The rate of persistence in improvement was calculated with $n = 63$ participants, who attended follow-up visits.

event, but also to multiple similar events. This raises an interesting question as to whether the language phrasing unique to AIT could efficiently process more than one event at a time. The observed reduction in the SUD score following an AIT session reflected improvements in the emotional intensity and the bodily sensation activated by the traumatic memory. Although these observations from therapists suggest clinical change, the nature of a self-reporting observational study does not allow for meaningful comparison with previously evaluated "gold standard modalities" nor does it allow for broad generalizability outside of the studied population.

It is notable, however, that study participants were clinicians practicing all over the globe, which suggests that, with further study, AIT may be applicable.

Limitations

To our knowledge, this is the first study to evaluate the potential effectiveness of AIT as a treatment modality for clearing negative emotions related to traumatic memories.

The study design did not allow for the establishment of a clear cause-and-effect relationship, but it provides a useful baseline for future, more rigorous studies. In particular, the degree to which the placebo effects and therapist allegiance bias may have led to the reported improvement in symptoms is not known. It is also possible that patients exaggerated the improvement of their symptoms for the purpose of pleasing the clinician, a known confounder in the evaluation of treatment efficacy (Blanchard & Farber, 2016). This effect cannot be assessed with this study design.

Most clinicians who responded to the survey reported completion of advanced coursework in AIT beyond the basic training module, which suggests that the respondents represent an adept group of clinicians with a significant degree of training in AIT in this dataset. Furthermore, most participants reported using AIT in the recent few months, thereby reducing the possible impact of recall bias on the study results. However, it is likely that clinicians who responded to the survey were enthusiastic about this treatment modality, a possible source of observer bias that must also be considered. A systematic review conducted by Lieb et al. (2016) evaluating 95 studies assessing the efficacy of various psychological interventions concluded that more than a quarter (27/95) evidenced some degree of observer bias. Likewise, the clinicians may have self-selected the most dramatically improved case to include in the survey, rather than an average case, a choice that would also exaggerate the positive effects reported in this study.

The methodology of the study, as a retrospective survey, allows for no ability to make causal inferences or suggest effect sizes. The survey focused on the clinicians' experiences with AIT's efficacy within their clinical practice, and thus, the selection criteria for clients was naturalistic rather than randomized, and there are no direct responses from the clients in terms of their subjective experiences.

An artifact of the process of AIT is that an emotional response should be treated to a SUD score of 0 or 1 in order to consider that event effectively treated. Should the SUD rating not reach either of these scores, AIT technique ideally is repeated until the score is adequately reduced. This may require anywhere from one to five "rounds" of intervention within a therapeutic session based upon the survey results. Thus, it does not make rational sense to "measure" SUD reduction in a single "round" of treatment, or to have expected therapists following the protocol to have documented such. The outcome of 0 or 1 SUD score was assessed not to create an expectation of success or a bias in that direction, but rather to adhere to the AIT standardized treatment protocol. This endpoint is also consistent with research and clinical practice measures used in EMDR.

There are a number of unique elements within the AIT treatment model, such as the specific wording of the therapeutic phrase or the chakra simulation. Given that the present study comprised a retrospective design, it is unclear which element of AIT, or combination thereof, produced the observed therapeutic effects. The hand placement over various energy centers, the verbal phrasing stated at each step, or some other factor could be studied independently in the future to analyze the relative contribution of each element.

Overall, therapists' assessments from this pilot study support the utility of AIT intervention to target and potentially improve emotional distress associated with past trauma. Although the retrospective study design did not allow for a clear cause-and-effect relationship, it provided a useful baseline for future, more rigorous studies. Future plans extending from this pilot study will include a randomized controlled trial to compare the therapeutic efficacy of AIT to that of the more widely studied and utilized energy psychology intervention, EFT.

Conclusions

Although this pilot study was limited to clinician observations of the ability of AIT to reduce the negative emotions related to past traumatic events, the initial data were supportive of potential clinical utility with this energy psychology technique. Additional studies are needed in the form of randomized controlled trials to evaluate more objectively this energy psychology intervention compared to those already recognized as clinically effective.

References

Advanced Integrative Institute. (2021). *Introduction: How it came to be.* Retrieved from https://ait.institute/intro-to-ait/

American Psychological Association. (2021). *Society of Clinical Psychology.* Retrieved from https://www.apa.org/about/division/div12

Association for Comprehensive Energy Psychology. (2021). *What is energy psychology and why should you care?* Retrieved from https://www.energypsych.org/page/aboutenergypsych

Bach, D., Groesbeck, G., Stapleton, P., Sims, R., Blickheuser, K., & Church, D. (2019). Clinical EFT (Emotional Freedom Techniques) improves multiple physiological markers of health. *Journal of Evidence-Based Integrative Medicine, 24.* doi:10.1177/2515690X18823691

Batra, K., Sharma, M., Batra, R., Singh, T. P., & Schvaneveldt, N. (2021). Assessing the psychological impact of COVID-19 among college students: An evidence of 15 countries. *Healthcare (Basel), 9*(2), 222. doi:10.3390/healthcare9020222

Batra, K., Singh, T. P., Sharma, M., Batra, R., & Schvaneveldt, N. (2020). Investigating the psychological impact of COVID-19 among healthcare workers: A meta-analysis. *International Journal of Environmental Research and Public Health, 17*(23), 9096. doi:10.3390/ijerph17239096

Bell, M. L., Whitehead, A. L., & Julious, S. A. (2018). Guidance for using pilot studies to inform the design of intervention trials with continuous outcomes. *Clinical Epidemiology, 10,* 153–157. doi:10.2147/CLEP.S146397

Billingham, S. A., Whitehead, A. L., & Julious, S. A. (2013). An audit of sample sizes for pilot and feasibility trials being undertaken in the United Kingdom registered in the United Kingdom Clinical Research Network database. *BMC Medical Research Methodology, 13*(1), 104. doi:10.1186/1471-2288-13-104

Blanchard, M., & Farber, B. A. (2016). Lying in psychotherapy: Why and what clients don't tell their therapist about therapy and their relationship. *Counselling Psychology Quarterly, 29*(1), 90–112. doi:10.1080/09515070.2015.1085365

Callahan, R. J. (2001). Raising and lowering of heart rate variability: Some clinical findings of Thought Field Therapy. *Journal of Clinical Psychology, 4*(4), 1175–1186. doi:10.1002/jclp.1084

Church, D., Stapleton, P., Kip, K., & Gallo, F. (2020). Corrigendum to: Is tapping on acupuncture points an active ingredient in Emotional Freedom Techniques: A systematic review and meta-analysis of comparative studies. *Journal of Nervous and Mental Disease, 208*(8), 632–635. doi:10.1097/NMD.0000000000001222.

Clinton, A. (2010). *Advanced Integrative Therapy: The Basics.* Advanced Integrative Therapy.

Clond, M. (2016). Emotional Freedom Techniques for Anxiety: for anxiety: A systematic review with meta-analysis. *Journal of Nervous and Mental Disease, 204*(5), 388–395. doi:10.1097/NMD.0000000000000483

Craig, G., & Fowlie, A. (1995). *Emotional Freedom Techniques: The manual.* Gary Craig.

Craik, F. I., Govoni, R., Naveh-Benjamin, M., & Anderson, N. D. (1996). The effects of divided attention on encoding and retrieval processes in human memory. *Journal of Experimental Psychology. General, 125*(2), 159–180. doi:10.1037/0096-3445.125.2.159

Dincer, B., & Inangil, D. (2021). The effect of Emotional Freedom Techniques on nurses' stress, anxiety, and burnout levels during the COVID-19 pandemic: A randomized controlled trial. *Explore: The Journal of Science and Healing, 17*(2), 109–114. doi:10.1016/j.explore.2020.11.012

Engebretson, J., & Wardell, D. W. (2007). Energy-based modalities. *Nursing Clinics of North America, 42*(2), 243–259. doi:10.1016/j.cnur.2007.02.004

Feinstein, D. (2021). Six empirically-supported premises about energy psychology: Mounting evidence for a controversial therapy. *Advances in Mind-Body Medicine, 35*(2), 17–32.

Inangil, D., Vural, P., Dogan, S., & Korpe, G. (2020). Effectiveness of music therapy and EmotionalFreedom Technique on test anxiety in Turkish nursing students: A randomised controlled trial. *European Journal of Integrative Medicine, 33.* doi:10.1016/j.eujim.2019.101041

Khan, A. M., Dar, S., Ahmed, R., Bachu, R., Adnan, M., & Kotapati, V. P. (2018). Cognitive Behavioral Therapy versus Eye Movement Desensitization and Reprocessing in patients with post-traumatic stress disorder: Systematic review and meta-analysis of randomized clinical trials. *Curēus (Palo Alto, CA), 10*(9), e3250–e3250. doi:10.7759/cureus.3250

Kolacz, J., Kovacic, K. K., & Porges, S. W. (2019). Traumatic stress and the autonomic brain-gut connection in development: Polyvagal Theory as an integrative framework for psychosocial and gastrointestinal pathology. *Developmental Psychobiology, 61*(5), 796–809. doi:10.1002/dev.21852

König, N., Steber, S., Seebacher, J., von Prittwitz, Q., Bliem, H. R., & Rossi, S. (2019). How therapeutic tapping can alter neural correlates of emotional prosody processing in anxiety. *Brain Sciences, 9*(8), 206. doi:10.3390/brainsci9080206

Lee, J. L. C., Nader, K., & Schiller, D. (2017). An update on memory reconsolidation updating. *Trends in Cognitive Sciences, 21*(7), 531–545. doi:10.1016/j.tics.2017.04.006

Lieb, K., von der Osten-Sacken, J., Stoffers-Winterling, J., Reiss, N., & Barth, J. (2016). Conflicts of interest and spin in reviews of psychological therapies: A systematic review. *BMJ Open, 6*(4), e010606. doi:10.1136/bmjopen-2015-010606

Mehdipour, A., Abedi, P., Ansari, S., & Dastoorpoor, M. (2021, May). The effectiveness of emotional freedom techniques (EFT) on depression of postmenopausal women: A randomized controlled trial. *Journal of Complementary and Integrative Medicine, 2021.* doi:10.1515/jcim-2020-0245

Moga, M. (2022). Is there scientific evidence for chakras? *International Journal of Healing and Caring, 22*(2), 39–45.

Morris J. A., Leclerc, C. M., & Kensinger, E. A. (2014). Effects of valence and divided attention on cognitive reappraisal processes. *Social Cognitive and Affective Neuroscience, 9*(12), 1952–1961. doi:10.1093/scan/nsu004

Santomauro, M. H., Mantilla Herrera, A. M., Shadid, J., Zheng, P., Ashbaugh, C., Pigott, D. M., … Deen, A. (2021). Global prevalence and burden of depressive and anxiety disorders in 204 countries and territories in 2020 due to the COVID-19 pandemic. *Lancet, 398*(10312), 1700–1712. doi:10.1016/S0140-6736(21)02143-7

Sebastian, B., & Nelms, J. (2017). The effectiveness of Emotional Freedom Techniques in the treatment of posttraumatic stress disorder: A meta-analysis. *Explore:*

The Journal of Science and Healing, 13(1), 16–25. doi:10.1016/j.explore.2016.10.001

Viechtbauer, W., Smits, L., Kotz, D., Budé, L., Spigt, M., Serroyen, J., & Crutzen, R. (2015). A simple formula for the calculation of sample size in pilot studies. *Journal of Clinical Epidemiology, 68*(11), 1375–1379. doi:10.1016/j.jclinepi.2015.04.014

Weaver, T. B. (2021). The use of Advanced Integrative Therapy with C-PTSD and intergenerational trauma transmission. *Energy Psychology: Theory, Research, and Treatment, 13*(2), 23–38. doi:10.9769/EPJ.2021.13.2.TBW

Whitehead, A. L., Julious, S. A., Cooper, C. L., & Campbell, M. J. (2016). Estimating the sample size for a pilot randomised trial to minimise the overall trial sample size for the external pilot and main trial for a continuous outcome variable. *Statistical Methods in Medical Research, 25*(3), 1057–1073. doi:10.1177/0962280215588241

Wolpe, J. (1973). *The practice of behavior therapy* (2d ed.). Pergamon Press.

Research on Acupoint Tapping Therapies Proliferating around the World

John Freedom, Santa Rosa, California USA
Marg Hux, Burlington, Ontario, Canada
Jan Warner, Veteran Affairs Medical Center, Cleveland, Ohio USA

Abstract

Background: The evidence base for acupoint tapping including Emotional Freedom Techniques (EFT) includes over 120 clinical trials showing relatively rapid and durable improvements for a range of psychological and physical conditions. It supports the premise that tapping is an active ingredient and shows associated physiologic changes. This evidence is based in standard Western literature databases such as EBSCO and overwhelmingly in English.

Objective: The current report explores international and regional research on EFT not previously known in the Western literature evidence base.

Methods and Results: A search of ResearchGate found 86 research studies on acupoint tapping not identified in standard Western databases. A systematic search of 21 databases using the EBSCO search engine yielded an additional five previously unknown papers for a total of 91 research studies. These studies were published in regional and international journals (71% in Indonesia) with most published primarily in languages other than English (81% had only title and/or abstract available in English). EFT was used in 47% of the studies, and the remaining studies used "Spiritual EFT" (SEFT), a variation developed in Indonesia combining tapping with spiritual affirmations from the Quran. The majority (84%) were single group or comparative clinical trials and 5% were literature reviews. The target issue included a range of psychological or medical conditions such as anxiety (29%), depression (15%), and hypertension (11%). In a further step, the potential magnitude of this additional research base was explored using Google Scholar. Challenges include inconsistent quality of translations, limited search capabilities of Google Scholar, lack of full text translated into English, and reasons why this literature is not found in the major databases.

Conclusion: This review identified a large number of studies that had been "invisible" in the West due to their having been published in non-English-language journals. They demonstrate growing interest in EFT throughout the world. In comparison with English-language EFT databases, these studies tend to be more frequently performed in treatment settings such as hospitals, clinics, and universities, and they often address medical diagnoses such as diabetes, hypertension, and pain as well as psychological conditions. In addition, they apply EFT with populations rarely focused upon in Western EFT studies, such as prisoners, addicts, cancer patients, and diabetics. Finally, these studies provide a valuable perspective on how acupoint tapping is being used around the world in real-life settings.

Keywords: tapping, EFT, Emotional Freedom Techniques, energy psychology, acupoint tapping, Spiritual EFT

John Freedom, CEHP, is a counselor and EFT practitioner and trainer in private practice in Santa Rosa, California. Author of *Heal Yourself with Emotional Freedom Technique*, he is the research committee chair for the Association for Comprehensive Energy Psychology (ACEP), serves on the board of trustees for EFT International, and is executive director of Finding Recovery and Empowerment from Abuse (FREA). **Marg Hux**, MSc, DipSP, is a registered psychotherapist in Toronto with a private practice using EFT and spiritual modalities. For 25 years she worked as a health economics researcher assessing the cost-effectiveness of different therapies in health care systems. **Jan Warner**, LISWS, PhD, is a clinical social worker affiliated with the Department of Social Work Services, Veterans Affairs Medical Center in Cleveland, Ohio. She is interested in the applications of EFT to reduce symptoms of fibromyalgia as well as in applications of energy psychology in low- and middle-income countries. **Correspondence:** John Freedom, CEHP, 8901 Oak Trail Drive, Santa Rosa, CA 95409; email: freejjii@gmail.com. **Disclosures:** John Freedom derives income from the practice of the methods described in this article. Marg Hux derives income from the practice of EFT. Jan Warner declares no conflict of interest.

Emotional Freedom Techniques (EFT) and Thought Field Therapy (TFT) are two modalities within the relatively new therapeutic approach known as energy psychology. EFT and TFT, together referred to as "acupoint tapping protocols," are evidence based, as examined in more than 300 peer-reviewed journal articles, including 120 clinical trials.

This evidence base as described by Feinstein (2021) shows that acupoint tapping results in improvements for a range of psychological conditions (anxiety, depression, phobias, anger, posttraumatic stress disorder [PTSD], chronic pain, concentration difficulties, stress, food cravings, insomnia, and performance blocks) and physical conditions (fibromyalgia, frozen shoulder, obesity, pain, psoriasis, and headaches). Recent independent meta-analyses confirm benefits for three common psychological conditions: anxiety (Clond, 2016), depression (Nelms & Castel, 2016), and PTSD (Sebastian & Nelms, 2017). All but two of the 120 clinical trials reported statistically significant improvement in at least one of the target outcomes (Feinstein, 2021). Additionally, the research shows that results are relatively rapid (compared to other therapies) and durable, with benefits retained on follow-up of 30 days to two years.

Although some skeptics have suggested that the tapping is an inconsequential artifact, six studies and a meta-analysis have shown that tapping is an active ingredient in the process (Church & Gallo, 2018). EFT and TFT are mind-body psychosensory techniques that produce measurable biological changes on physiological assessments including cardiovascular function (heart rate variability [HRV], resting heart rate, blood pressure), immune function (e.g. immunoglobulin A, increased lymphocyte production), and the stress hormone cortisol (Babamahmoodi et al., 2015; Bach et al., 2019). Brain scan studies using qEEG and fMRI have shown that these protocols increase or decrease arousal in specific areas of the brain (Feinstein, 2021). Additionally, the magnitude of clinical change and brevity of treatment suggest substantial healthcare cost savings (Church, 2010), and tapping described as "combined cognitive and somatic therapies" has been shown to be cost-effective compared to other standard treatments for PTSD (Mavranezouli, 2020).

In late 2020, the first author (JF) identified a body of additional EFT research not part of the recognized evidence base, which includes research studies published in English in Western journals and indexed in major search engines such as Scopus, EBSCO, PsycInfo, and PubMed. These additional studies were identified through Research Gate (researchgate.com). With a subsequent search of reference lists of the initial papers, a total of 86 research papers of tapping therapies not indexed in the major search engines were identified. These papers included clinical studies using single group or control group designs for psychological or medical issues and several literature reviews of the research related to acupoint tapping therapies. A substantial number used a specific form of EFT called "Spiritual EFT" (SEFT), a variation of EFT developed by Ahmad Faiz Zainuddin of Indonesia that combines tapping with spiritual affirmations from the Quran (Zainuddin, 2008).

The existence of this body of additional research was considered to be potentially significant since it may be larger than the previously known evidence base. Further exploration of this additional body of research was undertaken.

Locating studies beyond those available through indexed literature databases, however, held some challenges in using replicable methods of evidence review and synthesis. Many published research studies are not available within the major indexed databases, as databases such as PubMed include only journals that have applied and met strict criteria. For articles that are indexed, there are powerful search engines with capabilities to facilitate identifying, classifying, and extracting information from literature on a specific review topic.

To find literature not within these indexed databases, web searching tools can provide a much wider range of information, including published studies in regional journals or dissertations. Google Scholar, for instance, is one web searching tool for research that uses internet crawler algorithms to find a wider range of scholarly papers located on journal hosting platforms, university libraries, and personal websites.

Objective

The current study is an exploration of the growing number and kinds of acupoint tapping research studies conducted and published in professional journals that are outside the standard evidence base, as well as the challenges in finding and identifying such research.

Methods

This exploration considered initial reports of research studies of acupoint tapping protocols EFT or TFT, collectively labeled "energy psychology" including any of the following designs: comparative clinical trials (randomized or not), single cohort studies assessing outcomes before and after treatment (cohort pre/post), case series, or qualitative studies. Literature reviews (systematic or comparative reviews) of acupoint tapping protocols were also considered eligible. As the purpose of this review was to explore some of the additional research not currently known, only studies not in the current known evidence base were considered. Studies published in any language were considered eligible.

An initial search of the EBSCO database system was conducted to identify if there were any further studies not previously identified, with a focus on publications not in English by excluding English papers where this was possible within the member databases of EBSCO. The authors selected the search data criteria as follows: articles published between 2000 and 2021 with the following search phrases in the title and/or abstract: "Emotional Freedom Technique," "Emotional Freedom Techniques," "Energy Psychology," "Thought Field Therapy," and "Spiritual EFT." The search was conducted on October 2, 2021, on 21 relevant databases offered by EBSCO.

Screening of articles based on title and abstract was conducted to identify eligible research studies or literature reviews not in the currently known evidence base. Editorial opinions and interviews were excluded. We included combined treatments where EFT, TFT, or SEFT were studied as a mixed treatment with another intervention such as meditation.

The body of research identified both from this systematic review and informally was then combined for our full set (Freedom, 2022). These were reviewed to abstract relevant characteristics. Information available in English (titles and citations) was used insofar as possible, and additional web searching was conducted for locations of treatment or study settings. Articles were classified with regard to country of the research/publication, English language availability (none, title only, title and abstract, full text), study design, energy psychology modality (EFT, TFT, SEFT), combination with other modality, comparator, study setting (medical, educational, community, forensic), population, target issue, sample size, and whether the study reported a significant benefit/effect. As many papers had only the title and abstract available in English, and we did not attempt to translate content from the original language, some of these factors were unclear.

In a subsequent step, broad web searching via Google Scholar with the same search terms was used to explore the potential magnitude, location, and types of additional research that might exist in regional medical journals.

Results

The EBSCO database search identified 171 results using the abstract search and 128 results using the title search, with most of the studies being found in four databases: Medline, Medline Complete, APA PsycInfo, and CINAHL Plus. After screening and removing duplicates, five additional eligible publications were found and added to the articles identified by the first author for a full set of 91 articles.

Appendices A and B provide a table of the study and clinical characteristics for each of the included studies and a list of the citations for each. Table 1 summarizes the country, English availability, and study types.

The majority (71%) of studies were conducted in Indonesia or published in Indonesian professional journals, with Korea (8%) and India (5%) the next most frequent, and the remaining studies representing a range of other countries. For most (81%), only abstract and/or title information was available in English and few full texts were in English. The majority (84%) were single group or comparative clinical trials. Of the 45 comparative studies, 41 (91%) did not state in the available information that the control was an active comparator, and so this was designated to be a "No tapping" comparator. Active comparison interventions included autogenic relaxation, fingerhold relaxation technique, music or singing, meditative walking, or a teaching intervention.

Table 1. *Study Characteristics*

Total	N	%
Country	91	
Indonesia	65	71.4%
Korea	7	7.7%
India	5	5.5%
China	2	2.2%
Iran	2	2.2%
Malaysia	2	2.2%
Other*	7	7.7%
Unclear	1	1.1%
English availability	91	
Title only	4	4.4%
Title & abstract	70	76.9%
Full text	17	18.7%
Type of Study	91	
Literature review	5	5.5%
Case series or case study	6	6.6%
Qualitative	4	4.4%
Cohort pre/post	31	34.1%
Comparative clinical trial**	45	49.5%

Note. *One paper (1.1%) was found for each of: Colombia, Gaza, Germany, Pakistan, Spain, Turkey, and Australia. **Comparative (controlled) trials may have been randomized and this was not always clear from abstract.

Table 2. *Study Clinical Characteristics*

Total	N	%
Treatment Modality		
EFT	43	47.3%
SEFT	48	52.7%
Study Treatment Setting		
Medical	36	39.1%
Community	14	15.2%
Educational	11	12.0%
Forensic	3	3.3%
Unclear	23	25.0%
N/A (review article)	5	5.4%
Target issue		
Anxiety	27	29.7%
Depression	14	15.4%
Hypertension	10	11.0%
Pain	8	8.8%
Quality of life	7	7.7%
Aggressiveness	3	3.3%
Negative emotions	4	4.4%
Insomnia	3	3.3%
Cognition	2	2.2%
Fatigue	2	2.2%
PTSD symptoms	2	2.2%
Schizophrenia symptoms	2	2.2%
Smoking	2	2.2%
Other*	5	5.5%
Clinical benefit (in clinical studies)**		
Yes	64	84.2%
Between groups nonsignificant	4	5.3%
Unclear	8	10.5%

Note. *Other includes "any condition" (review study), family functioning, spiritual perception, hypertension, blood sugar, and "qualitative experience of EFT." **For the 76 studies reporting trial (single cohort, comparative, randomized trial).

Table 2 shows the study modalities, settings, target issues, and whether clinical benefit was reported.

The SEFT modality was reported for 53% of the studies; remaining studies were of EFT. There were no TFT (Thought Field Therapy) studies found.

The most frequent primary target issues were the psychological issues of anxiety (30%), depression (15%), and the medical issue of hypertension (11%). Participants included medical or psychiatric patients (anxiety and depression being the most frequent diagnoses). Other groups included prisoners, those employed, those with substance abuse, and even a population described as "introverted and extroverted personality types." The population of participants drew from many ages including children, university students, and the elderly.

Considering the clinical trials (single group or comparative), 84% stated in the abstract that there was a clinical benefit of tapping. Most studies had small sample sizes, and of the 30 cohort pre/post studies reporting a sample size in their abstract, 21 (70%) had less than 30 participants (range 5–23) while 9 (30%) had 30 or more (range 30–97). Of the 40 comparative studies (including RCTs) reporting a sample size in their abstract, 35 (87.5%) had less than 60 participants allowing approximately 30 per group (range 7–52) while only 5 (12.5%) had 60 or more (range 60–100).

Explorations were conducted of the feasibility of systematic searching using a web-based search engine, Google Scholar (GS). A search for these same terms (as of November 19, 2021) identified 7,890 scholarly papers. GS allows search by several identified languages, and of these, 5,670 were published in English and 778 had other identified language of: German (180), Spanish (155), French (154), Japanese (55), Korean (54), Portuguese (47), Dutch (38), Italian (38), Turkish (34), Chinese (16), or Polish (7). From an inspection of titles and abstracts for several European languages, most identified papers were discussions of tapping protocols and their relevance in local clinical practice, and not reports of new research. None of the Dutch papers were relevant to our exploration.

As it is not possible in Google Scholar to identify papers excluding specific languages, although we can assume that there are approximately 1,420 in another non-English language, it is not possible to identify a list of those for more specific screening.

Conducting a GS search for "spiritual emotional freedom technique" yielded 926 results and limiting to English yielded 224 results. A visual inspection of the English-language papers showed that there are additional studies documenting the effectiveness of SEFT, most of which originated in Indonesia.

Discussion

We describe here a set of 91 research studies not previously part of the Western literature evidence base for acupoint tapping therapies and have identified the potential existence of a large number of additional studies in additional countries. Beyond the research discovered informally, an EBSCO database search confirmed that very few of these were included in the standard indexed databases.

The studies include both EFT and Spiritual EFT modalities in a wide range of countries with Asian countries and Indonesia particularly being the most frequent. The research was mostly (84%) single group or comparative trials, and for most, only title and abstract were available in English.

Compared to the Western body of evidence, these studies considered similar target issues in some regards, with the most frequently addressed issues being anxiety and depression, both considered to meet criteria for being evidence based (Feinstein, 2021). Medical issues and settings were well represented in this body of research, with medical being the most frequent setting type, and medical issues (e.g., hypertension or women's health) a frequent target. This is in contrast to the Western body of meridian tapping research which focuses primarily on psychological issues. Most comparative studies only stated in the abstract that they had a control group, and this was assumed to be a "no tapping" comparator for our summary. Similarly, a high proportion (84%) stated there was a clinical benefit.

A high proportion of the research found was conducted in Indonesia and used the EFT variation SEFT, which, as noted, carries a religious connotation and refers to combining tapping acupoint points with reciting verses from the Quran and surrendering to the Will of Allah. Considering the 65 Indonesian studies, 44 used the Spiritual EFT modality; SEFT studies were also found in India, Malaysia, and Spain for a total of 48 SEFT studies. Adding spirituality to healing is consistent with an Indonesian emphasis on spirituality in other aspects of society; for example, citizens are required to specify their religious affiliation on identification cards. Thus, SEFT is a psychospiritual as well as a psychosensory technique.

This exploration of local or regional scientific research on acupoint tapping was challenging. Local and regional scientific journals are not indexed in the international databases, which have quite strict inclusion criteria. Journal editors aiming to be included in such a database submit a formal application providing supporting evidence that is reviewed by scientific committees considering quality of the scientific content, principles of publication ethics, and author consent, and including a peer review process. Criteria include the research impact measured as number of citations within the major databases, which is difficult to meet without being indexed and constitutes a "Catch-22" (Bordons & Gomez, 2004). Additionally, regional journals are often published primarily in the local language of the medical community, and even when included in the indexed databases, English full text may not be available. Standard practice in systematic searching is to exclude non-English-language papers, and such exclusion is considered to have no impact on the final conclusions (Jackson & Kuriyama, 2019). A review of 250 systematic reviews for traditional medical topics found that only 22% included any non-English-language papers, and in those, the non-English papers formed 2% of the total evidence base (Jackson & Kuriyama, 2019). Meta-analyses and systematic reviews investigating the effect on the conclusions of excluding publications in languages other than English found no evidence of systematic bias in the results. (Dobrescu et al., 2021; Morrison et al., 2012).

Strengths and Limitations

This paper has identified that a body of research on the effectiveness of tapping protocols exists outside of and potentially larger than the (primarily Western) previously known research. These studies relate to local medical and psychological practice in Asian countries and regional academic journals. Although for most papers only abstract information was available, 84% of studies reported a clinical benefit of the tapping protocol for a variety of target issues, populations, and settings. Similar to other EFT research, most studies used relatively small sample sizes of 30 or fewer.

Strengths of these studies include the following: most of the studies were conducted at clinics, hospitals, and/or universities. In addition to the common psychological issues of anxiety, depression, stress, and PTSD, research studies explored EP effectiveness for addictions, aggression, burnout, self-acceptance, learning concentration, schizophrenia, and overall mental health. Many documented the effectiveness of acupoint tapping for medical conditions (e.g., diabetes, fatigue, hypertension, insomnia, and menstrual pain). Some documented effectiveness for psychological or medical conditions in specific populations (e.g., children, people with cancer, coronary heart disease, chronic kidney disease, drug addicts, elderly, female university students, HIV/AIDS, hemodialysis patients, pregnant women, prisoners, pulmonary tuberculosis, stroke patients, and women with breast cancer) Finally, these studies provide a valuable perspective on how acupoint tapping is being used around the world in real-life settings.

A major limitation of this review is that full English text was available for few research papers. For the majority of papers only the title and abstract were in English. Therefore, classifications of the major characteristics were not always present, and assumptions were used from brief statements. For example, whether a control was a wait list or no intervention, any follow-up, and magnitude of effects were often not known without the full English text.

Another limitation is that we describe studies identified from an informal search and a few additional ones found using a systematic search process of 22 databases in EBSCO, but not including SCOPUS, another possibly relevant database. We found that although a large body of potential additional research studies exists, it was beyond the scope of this review to screen the 7,890 citations in GS to identify research papers without the capabilities to remove duplicates and build a search strategy in the ways that the standard databases allow.

Based on website searches using GS, we found a large additional set of studies utilizing EFT and SEFT as interventions, with a large research base in Indonesia. (These research studies from Indonesia are potentially larger than those in all other countries combined!) However, since these are not represented in major publications databases, and Indonesian language studies are not indexed in Google Scholar, screening of the full set of potential results was beyond the scope of this exploration.

These limitations make it difficult to generalize the findings of this review to understand the full evidence outside the Western evidence base. Additional searching using GS with the large number of papers found using keywords would supplement this research set, even though GS lacks standard capabilities found in the major databases to conduct this search, which would therefore make this challenging.

Conclusion

Interest in EFT and EFT research continues to proliferate organically throughout the world. The current study used a categorical review process to examine the research evidence for cross-cultural efficacy of EFT and SEFT. It identified a large body of previously unknown research across a wide demographic range, with varied populations receiving benefit. As therapeutic interventions, EFT and SEFT show clinical value as cost-effective, non-pharmaceutical treatments for both psychological and some medical conditions, in a wide range of settings and demographics, in a large collection of targeted issues.

References

Babamahmoodi, A., Arefnasab, Z., Noorbala, A. A., Ghanei, M., Babamahmoodie, F., Alipour, A., ... Darabi, H. (2015). Emotional Freedom Technique (EFT) effects on psychoimmunological factors of chemically pulmonary injured veterans. *Iranian Journal of Allergy, Asthma and Immunology, 14*(1), 37–47.

Bach, D., Groesbeck, G., Stapleton, P., Banton, S., Blickheuser, K., & Church, D. (2019). Clinical EFT (Emotional Freedom Techniques) improves multiple physiological markers of health. *Journal of Evidence-Based Integrative Medicine, 24.* doi:1.1177/2515690X18823691

Bordons, M., & Gómez Caridad, I. (2004). Towards a single language in science? A Spanish view. Serials, *17*(2), 190–195.

Church, D. (2010). The economic cost savings of energy psychology treatment. *Energy Psychology: Theory, Research, and Treatment, 2*(1), 9–12.

Church, D., Stapleton, P., Yang, A., & Gallo, F. (2018). Is tapping on acupuncture points an active ingredient in Emotional Freedom Techniques (EFT)? A systematic review and meta-analysis of comparative studies. *Journal of Nervous and Mental Disease, 206*(10), 783–793. doi:10.1097/NMD.0000000000000878

Clond, M. (2016). Emotional Freedom Techniques for anxiety: A systematic review with meta-analysis. *Journal of Nervous and Mental Disease, 204*(5), 388–395. doi:10.1097/NMD.0000000000000483

Dobrescu, A. I., Nussbaumer, S. B., Klerings, I., Wagner, G., Persad, E., Sommer, I., ... Gartlehner, G. (2021). Restricting evidence syntheses of interventions to English-language publications is a viable methodological shortcut for most medical topics: A systematic review. *Journal of Clinical Epidemiology*, 137, 209–217.

Feinstein, D. (2021). Six empirically-supported premises about energy psychology: Mounting evidence for a controversial therapy. *Advances in Mind-Body Medicine, 35*(2), 17–32. Retrieved from https://advances-journal.com/wp-content/uploads/2021/05/Feinstein.pdf

Freedom, J. (2022). *EP research in non-English language journals.* Association for Comprehensive Energy Psychology. Retrieved from https://www.energypsych.org/researchdb8c71b7

Jackson, J. L., & Kuriyama, A. (2019). How often do systematic reviews exclude articles not published in English? *Journal of General Internal Medicine, 34*(8), 1388–1389. doi: 10.1007/s11606-019-04976-x

Mavranezouli, I., Megnin-Viggars, O., Grey, N., Bhutani, G., Leach, J., Daly, C., ... Pilling, S. (2020). Cost-effectiveness of psychological treatments for post-traumatic stress disorder in adults. *PloS One*, *15*(4), e0232245. doi: 10.1371/journal.pone.0232245

Morrison, A., Polisena, J., Husereau, D., Moulton, K., Clark, M., Fiander, M., ... Rabb, D. (2012). The effect of English-language restriction on systematic review-based meta-analyses: a systematic review of empirical studies. *International Journal of Technology Assessment in Health Care, 28*(2), 138–144.

Nelms, J., & Castel, D. (2016). A systematic review and meta-analysis of randomized and non-randomized trials of clinical Emotional Freedom Techniques (EFT) for the treatment of depression. *Explore: The Journal of Science and Healing, 12*(6), 416–426. doi:1.1016/j.explore.2016.08.001

Sebastian, B., & Nelms, J. (2017). The effectiveness of Emotional Freedom Techniques in the treatment of post-traumatic stress disorder: A meta-analysis. *Explore: The Journal of Science and Healing, 13*, 16–25. doi:1.1016/j.explore.2016.1.001

Zainuddin, A. F. (2008). *SEFT: Spiritual Emotional Freedom Technique.* East Jakarta, Indonesia: Afzan Publishing.

Appendix A: Table of Included Studies

Ref #	Author, Year	Country	English Available	Study Type	EP Modality	Comparator	Setting Type	Population	Target Issue	Sample Size
1	Wati et al., 2021	Indonesia	Full text	Comparative study	EFT	No tapping	Medical	Chronic kidney disease	Fatigue	19
2	Altuntas et al., 2020	Turkey	Title & abstract	Qualitative	EFT	N/A	unclear	Women	Other	21
3	Ardan et al., 2020	Indonesia	Title & abstract	Cohort pre/post	SEFT	None	unclear	HIV/AIDS adults	Depression	16
4	Asmawati et al., 2020	Indonesia	Full text	Cohort pre/post	SEFT	None	Community	NAPZA residents	Anxiety	18
5	Dewi & Fitri, 2020	Indonesia	Title & abstract	Qualitative	SEFT	N/A	Forensic	Prisoners	Depression	10
6	Dewi et al., 2020	Indonesia	Full text	Comparative study	EFT	No tapping	Medical	Post-stroke patients	QOL	46
7	Fachrin et al., 2020	Indonesia	Title & abstract	Comparative study	SEFT	No tapping	Community	Employed	Fatigue	38
8	Fitri, 2020	Indonesia	Title & abstract	RCT	EFT	No tapping	Community	Elderly	Anxiety	20
9	Isnadiya et al., 2020	Indonesia	Title & abstract	RCT	EFT	No tapping	Medical	Patients undergoing percutaneous coronary intervention	Anxiety	24
10	Lataima et al., 2020	Indonesia	Full text	Literature review	EFT	N/A	N/A	N/A	Anxiety	11
11	Muliani et al., 2020	Indonesia	Title & abstract	Cohort pre/post	EFT	None	Medical	Psychiatric patients	Aggressiveness	19
12	Permatasari et al., 2020	Indonesia	Title & abstract	Comparative study	SEFT	No tapping	Medical	Pregnant women with hypertension	Hypertension	15
13	Rahmadanti & Widyarini, 2020	Indonesia	Title & abstract	Cohort pre/post	EFT	None	Community	Victims of violence	Negative emotions	11
14	Setiyowati & Rahman, 2020	Indonesia	Title & abstract	Case study	SEFT	N/A	Medical	unclear	Anxiety	1
15	Susanto, 2020	Indonesia	Title & abstract	Comparative study	SEFT	No tapping	Medical	Patients	Pain	36
16	Trejos Parra et al., 2020	Colombia	Full text	Cohort pre/post	EFT	None	Community	Children with abuse-related PTSD	PTSD symptoms	37
17	Aftrinanto et al., 2019	Indonesia	Title & abstract	Cohort pre/post	SEFT	None	unclear	Women	QOL	6
18	Ali & Loona, 2019	Pakistan	Full text	Cohort pre/post	EFT	None	Educational	Female university students	Anxiety	70
19	Ardan et al., 2019	Indonesia	Full text	RCT	SEFT	No tapping	Medical	People living with HIV/AIDS	Depression	32
20	Begré, 2019	Germany	Title & abstract	Literature review	EFT	N/A	N/A	N/A	Anxiety	N/A
21	Fatmasari et al., 2019	Malaysia	Title & abstract	Cohort pre/post	SEFT	None	unclear	Hypertensive patients	Anxiety	5

(Continued)

Ref #	Author, Year	Country	English Available	Study Type	EP Modality	Comparator	Setting Type	Population	Target Issue	Sample Size
22	Hidayatullah et al., 2019	Indonesia	Title & abstract	RCT	SEFT	No tapping	Educational	Introverted and extroverted students	Anxiety	36
23	Isworo et al., 2019	Indonesia	Title & abstract	RCT	EFT	No tapping	Medical	Hypertensive patients on antihypertensive medication	Hypertension	32
24	Krishnamurthy & Sharma, 2019	India	Title & abstract	RCT	EFT	No tapping	Medical	Patients with depression	Depression	10
25	Lina et al., 2019	Indonesia	Title & abstract	RCT	SEFT	Autogenic relaxation	Medical	Hemodialysis patients	Anxiety	unclear
26	Lismayanti & Hidayatulloh, 2019	Indonesia	Title & abstract	RCT	SEFT	No tapping	unclear	Hypertensive patients	Hypertension	30
27	Liu et al., 2019	China	Title & abstract	RCT	EFT	No tapping	unclear	Elderly patients with coronary heart disease	Depression	52
28	Marwing, 2019	Indonesia	Title & abstract	Cohort pre/post	SEFT	None	Community	Adolescents being fostered	Aggressiveness	16
29	Prabowo, 2019	Indonesia	Title & abstract	Comparative study	SEFT	No tapping	Medical	Preoperative adults	Anxiety	60
30	Prabowo et al., 2019	Indonesia	Title & abstract	Comparative study	SEFT	No tapping	unclear	Congestive heart failure	Anxiety	40
31	Rosyanti et al., 2019	India	Full text	Comparative study	SEFT	No tapping	unclear	Adults with schizophrenia	Schizophrenia symptoms	20
32	Sonhaji & Lekatompessy, 2019	India	Title & abstract	Comparative study	SEFT	Singing	Community	Elderly	Hypertension	unclear
33	Susilowati et al., 2019	India	Title	Literature review	SEFT	N/A	N/A	N/A	Anxiety	na
34	Warni & Hayana, 2019	Indonesia	Title & abstract	Comparative study	SEFT	No tapping	Community	Adults	Hypertension	64
35	Wati et al., 2019	Indonesia	Full text	Comparative study	EFT	No tapping	Medical	Nurses	Negative emotions	38
36	Afriyanti & Wenni, 2018	Indonesia	Full text	Cohort pre/post	SEFT	None	Medical	Women with breast cancer	Depression	33
37	Hamidiyah & Jannah, 2018	Indonesia	Title & abstract	Cohort pre/post	SEFT	None	Medical	Females with dysmenorrhea	Pain	10
38	Huda & Alvita, 2018	Indonesia	Full text	Comparative study	SEFT	No tapping	unclear	Hypertensives	Hypertension	33
39	Kasron, 2018	Indonesia	Title & abstract	Comparative study	SEFT	Progressive muscle relaxation	unclear	Hypertensives	Insomnia	32

40	Khoeriyah et al., 2018	Indonesia	Title & abstract	Comparative study	EFT	No tapping	Forensic	Adolescent prisoners	Negative emotions	32
41	Komang et al., 2018	Indonesia	Title & abstract	Comparative study	EFT	No tapping	Educational	Adolescents	Cognition	30
42	Lismayanti, 2018	Indonesia	Full text	Cohort pre/post	SEFT	None	unclear	Adults < 65	Hypertension	30
43	Madoni et al., 2018	Indonesia	Title & abstract	Comparative study	EFT	Group counselling with systematic desensitization	Educational	Students	Anxiety	16
44	Mardjan et al., 2018	Indonesia	Title & abstract	Comparative study	EFT	No tapping	unclear	Pregnant adolescents	Anxiety	unclear
45	Ma'rifah et al., 2018	Indonesia	Title & abstract	Comparative study	SEFT	Fingerhold relaxation technique	Medical	Mothers	Pain	45
46	Navianti et al., 2018	Indonesia	Title & abstract	Comparative study	EFT	No tapping	Medical	Patients giving blood	Anxiety	65
47	Novitriani & Hidayati, 2018	Indonesia	Title & abstract	Comparative study	SEFT	No tapping	Forensic	Female prisoners	QOL	31
48	Patriyani & Rahayu, 2018	Indonesia	Title & abstract	Comparative study	SEFT	No tapping	Medical	Type 2 diabetics	Other	100
49	Puspita, 2018	Indonesia	Title & abstract	Cohort pre/post	SEFT	None	Educational	Young women	Pain	97
50	Rosyanti et al., 2018	Indonesia	Title & abstract	Comparative study	SEFT	No tapping	Medical	People living with schizophrenia	Schizophrenia symptoms	7
51	Sahlia et al., 2018	Indonesia	Title & abstract	Comparative study	EFT	No tapping	unclear	People with hypertension	Depression	20
52	Etika et al., 2017	Indonesia	Title & abstract	Comparative study	SEFT	Keroncong music	Medical	Elderly	Depression	20
53	Jhansi et al., 2017	unclear	Title & abstract	Comparative study	EFT	No tapping	unclear	unclear	Anxiety	unclear
54	Kartikasari et al., 2017	Indonesia	Title & abstract	Cohort pre/post	EFT	None	unclear	Elderly	Insomnia	23
55	Kim, 2017	Korea	Title	Case study	EFT	N/A	unclear	unclear	QOL	1
56	Kusnanto et al., 2017	Indonesia	Full text	Cohort pre/post	SEFT	None	unclear	People with tuberculosis	QOL	22
57	Lee et al., 2017	Korea	Title & abstract	Literature review	EFT	N/A	N/A	N/A	Anxiety	N/A
58	Liu et al., 2017	China	Title & abstract	Cohort pre/post	EFT	None	Medical	People with cancer	Depression	unclear
59	Soto-Vasquez & Alvarado-García, 2017	Spain	Title & abstract	Comparative study	EFT	No tapping	Educational	University students	Anxiety	48

(Continued)

Ref #	Author, Year	Country	English Available	Study Type	EP Modality	Comparator	Setting Type	Population	Target Issue	Sample Size
60	Sutiyarsih & Sri, 2017	Indonesia	Title & abstract	Cohort pre/post	EFT	None	unclear	Geriatric	Depression	30
61	Yuswinda, 2017	Indonesia	Title & abstract	Cohort pre/post	SEFT	None	Medical	Preop Patients	Anxiety	8
62	Faridah, 2016	Indonesia	Title & abstract	RCT	SEFT	No tapping	Medical	Blood pressure	Other	26
63	Kim et al., 2016	Korea	Title & abstract	Comparative study	EFT	Meditative walk	Community	Menopausal women	QOL	26
64	Ningsih et al., 2016	Malaysia	Title & abstract	Comparative study	EFT	No tapping	Medical	Breast cancer patients	Anxiety	30
65	Sastra & Sari, 2016	Indonesia	Title & abstract	Comparative study	EFT	No tapping	Educational	Adolescents	Pain	12
66	Wahyuliarmy, 2016	Indonesia	Title & abstract	Case study	SEFT	N/A	Community	63 -year-olds	Pain	1
67	Abdi & Abolmaali, 2015	Iran	Title & abstract	Comparative study	EFT	No tapping	Community	Single mothers	Aggressiveness	30
68	Astuti et al., 2015	Indonesia	Title & abstract	Cohort pre/post	SEFT	None	Medical	Women with HIV	Depression	30
69	Banerjee, 2015	India	Full text	Qualitative	EFT	N/A	Educational	University students	Depression	30
70	Etika & Wijaya, 2015	Indonesia	Title & abstract	Cohort pre/post	SEFT	None	Educational	Students of SMAN 5 Kediri City	Smoking	14
71	Ghamsari & Lavasani, 2015	Iran	Title & abstract	Comparative study	EFT	No tapping	Medical	Pregnant women	Anxiety	30
72	Hermanwan et al., 2015	Indonesia	Title & abstract	Comparative study	EFT	No tapping	Educational	Students	Cognition	unclear
73	Kartikodaru et al., 2015	Indonesia	Title & abstract	Cohort pre/post	SEFT	None	Medical	Receiving chemotherapy	Anxiety	17
74	Putra, 2015	Indonesia	Title & abstract	Case Study	SEFT	N/A	Medical	Parents of sexually abused child	Anxiety	1
75	Rofacky & Aini, 2015	Indonesia	Title & abstract	Comparative study	SEFT	No tapping	unclear	Hypertensives	Hypertension	30
76	Susanti, 2015	Indonesia	Title & abstract	Cohort pre/post	SEFT	None	Medical	Patients with hypertension	Hypertension	17
77	Wijaya, 2015	Indonesia	Title & abstract	Cohort pre/post	SEFT	None	unclear	Elderly patients with hypertension	Hypertension	16
78	Desmaniarti & Avianti, 2014	Indonesia	Title & abstract	RCT	SEFT	No tapping	Medical	Patients with cervical cancer	Anxiety	68
79	Latifah & Ramawati, 2014	Indonesia	Title & abstract	Comparative study	EFT	None	Medical	Women post Caesarian section	Pain	30
80	Lee et al., 2014	Korea	Title	Case series	EFT	N/A	unclear	unclear	Anxiety	unclear

81	MacKinnon, 2014	Australia	Full text	Case study	EFT	N/A	Community	People with trauma in family therapy	Other	2
82	Shari et al., 2014	Indonesia	Title & abstract	Cohort pre/post	EFT	None	Medical	Coronary patients	Anxiety	30
83	Song et al., 2014	Korea	Title	Qualitative	EFT	N/A	unclear	Hwa-byung (suppressed anger)	Negative emotions	13
84	Alwan & Nawajha, 2013	Gaza	Full text	Comparative study	EFT	No tapping	Community	Diabetic persons	QOL	36
85	Bakara et al., 2013	Indonesia	Title & abstract	Comparative study	SEFT	No tapping	Medical	Patients with coronary disease	Depression	42
86	Kim et al., 2013	Korea	Title & abstract	Literature review	EFT	N/A	N/A	N/A	Other	N/A
87	Mariyati & Habibah, 2013	Indonesia	Title & abstract	Cohort pre/post	SEFT	None	Educational	Junior high school students	Smoking	12
88	Safitri & Sadif, 2013	Indonesia	Full text	Cohort pre/post	SEFT	None	Medical	Renal hemodialysis patients	Depression	12
89	Ulfa, 2013	Indonesia	Title & abstract	RCT	SEFT	No tapping	unclear	Adolescent survivors of volcanic eruption	PTSD symptoms	22
90	Lee et al., 2011	Korea	Title & abstract	Cohort pre/post	EFT	None	Community	Elderly women	Insomnia	10
91	Hakam et al., 2009	Indonesia	Title & abstract	Cohort pre/post	SEFT	None	Medical	Cancer patients	Pain	20

Note. NAPZA = narcotics, psychotropics, and other addictive substances; QOL = quality of life.

Appendix B: List of Citations

1. Wati, N., Dewi, N., Meilena, N., & Lestari, R. (2021). Emotional Freedom Technique (EFT) therapy on chronic kidney disease (CKD) patients to reduce fatigue. *Jurnal Keperawatan, 12*(1). doi:10.22219/jk.v12i1.9763
2. Altuntas, S., & Duzguner, S. (2020). A qualitative research on individual, social and spiritual changes in women supported with Emotional Freedom Technique. *Ankara Üniversitesi İlahiyat Fakültesi Dergisi, 61*(2), 453–492. Q10:S49
3. Ardan, M., Zulkifli, A., & Jafar, N. (2020). Therapy SEFT for controlling the level of depression in people with HIV and AIDS. *Enfermeria Clinica, 30*(4), 444–447.
4. Asmawati, Ikhlasia, M., & Panduragan, S. L. (2020). The effect of Spiritual Emotional Freedom Technique (SEFT) therapy on the anxiety of NAPZA (narcotics, psychotropic, and other addictive substances) residents. *Enfermeria Clinica, 30*(Suppl 5), 206–208.
5. Dewi, I., & Fitri, S. (2020). Utilization of SEFT as a community therapy model (TC) for mental and spiritual health of drug addicts. *Jurnal Pengabdian Untuk Munege RI, 4*(1).
6. Dewi, N. L., Arifin, M., & Ismail, S. (2020). The influence of Gayatri Mantra and Emotional Freedom Technique on quality of life of post-stroke patients. *Journal of Multidisciplinary Healthcare, 13,* 909–916. doi:10.2147/JMDH.S266580 Corpus ID: 221880595
7. Fachrin, S., Amelia, A., Rizki, A., & Farinah, K. (2020). The effectiveness of Spiritual Emotional Freedom Technique (SEFT) therapy against the reduction of work fatigue in PT WIKA Beton Makassar. *International Journal of Science and Healthcare Research, 5*(3), ss.338–344. Website: ijshr.com. Research Paper ISSN: 2455-7587
8. Fitri, R. (2020). The effectiveness of EFT to reduce anxiety in the face of degenerative disease in the elderly viewed from social support. *Al Ulya: Journal of Islamic Education, 5*(1), 52–66.
9. Isnadiya, A., Risca, F., Taufiq, R., & Utomo, P. (2019). The effect of Emotional Freedom Technique (EFT) on anxiety levels of pre percutaneous coronary intervention (PCI) patients. *Jurnal Ilmu Keperawatan Medikal Bedah, 1*(2). doi:10.32584/jikmb.v1i2.187
10. Lataima, N., Kurniawati, N., & Astuti, P. (2020). Benefits of Emotional Freedom Technique (EFT) for patients with anxiety disorders. *Jurnal Penelitian Kesehatan Suara Forikes, 11*(2).
11. Muliani, R., Abidin, I., & Adawiyah, R. (2020). The effect of Emotional Freedom Technique on aggressive levels of risk behavior. *Jurnal Keperawatan, 'Aisyiyah, 6*(2).
12. Permatasari, A., Pujiastuti, E., & Mulyantoro, D. (2020). Spiritual Emotional Freedom Technique (SEFT) intervention on blood pressure among pregnancy with hypertension. *International Journal of Nursing and Health Services, 3*(3), 402–410.
13. Rahmadanti, D., & Widyarini, N. (2020). The effectiveness of Hypno-EFT (Emotional Freedom Technique) to reduce negative emotions in women victims of violence. *International Journal of Research Publications, 46*(1).
14. Setiyowati, E., & Rahman, A. (2020). Application of spiritual freedom emotional technique (SEFT) therapy for tuberculosis patients with nursing problems at the Sawahan Health Center. *Journal of Health Science, 13*(1).
15. Susanto, M. (2020). Effectiveness of SEFT Therapy on post op laparotomy pain in the operating room at RSI Agung Semarang. *Medicalia Hospitalia, 7*(1), 59–63.
16. Trejos Parra, J. J., García Osorio, C. L., Vélez Vitola, O., & Muñoz García, M. (2020). Effectiveness of emotional freedom techniques with a recreational plastic expression program in post-traumatic stress of school age children boarded for abuse-related trauma. *Psicología Desde El Caribe, 37*(1), 75–98.
17. Aftrinanto, Z., Hayati, E. N. N., & Urbayatun, S. (2018). Spiritual Emotional Freedom Techniques (SEFT) improves quality of life in women experiencing a landslide disaster. *Jurnal Studia Insania, 6*(1), 069–089. doi:10.18592/jsi.v6i1.2006
18. Ali, S. A-E-Z., Loona, M. I. (2019). Effectiveness of tapping therapy for the treatment of anxiety among university students. *Pakistan Journal of Physiology, 15*(2), 80–83.
19. Ardan., M., Zulkifli, A., & Jafar, N. (2019). The combination between Spiritual Therapy and Emotional Freedom Technique to control the depression level in people with HIV and AIDS at Samarinda City. *European Journal of Research in Medical Science, 7*(1), 28–35.
20. Begré, S. (2019). [Touching the soul—Energy psychology in psychosomatics]. *Therapeutische Umschau. Revue Therapeutique, 76*(5), 252–260. doi:10.1024/0040-5930/a001089
21. Fatmasari, D., Widyana, R., & Budiyani, K. (2019). Spiritual Emotional Freedom Technique to reduce stress in hypertensive patients. *Jurnal Psikologi, 15*(1), 10–19.
22. Hidayatullah, R., Noviekayati, I., & Saragih, S. (2019). The effectiveness of Spiritual Emotional Freedom Technique to reduce new santri anxiety reviewed from the personality type. *PSIKOSAINS (Journal of Psychology Research and Thought), 13*(2), 144–156.
23. Isworo, A., Anam, A., & Indrawati, N. (2019). Effects of Emotional Freedom Technique therapy on reducing blood pressure in elderly hypertension. *Gaster Jurnal Kesehatan, 17*(2). doi:10.30787/gaster.v17i2.438
24. Krishnamurthy, D., & Sharma, A. (2019). Effectiveness of Emotional Freedom Techniques: A pilot study. *Indian Journal of Public Health Research and Development, 10*(10). doi:10.5958/0976-5506.2019.02836
25. Lina, L., Sabriyanti, H., & Sartika, A. (2019). Decreased the anxiety scale of hemodialysis patients with the Spiritual Emotional Freedom Technique (SEFT) and Autogenic Relaxation. *Southeast Asia Nursing Research, 1*(3), 142–147.
26. Lismayanti, L., & Hidayatulloh, B. (2019). Spiritual Emotional Freedom Technique (SEFT) therapy reduces blood pressure in hypertension patients. *Journal of Nursing and Health, 2*(1), 15–26. doi:10.25099/jnh.Vol2.Iss1.23
27. Wanying, L., Ruihua, J., Jingmeng, N., & Xiao, Z. (2019). Effect of emotional freedom techniques on anxiety and depression in elderly patients with coronary heart disease. *Nursing of Integrated Traditional Chinese and Western Medicine, 5*(8), 123–125.
28. Marwing, A. (2019). Effectiveness of SEFT (Spiritual Emotional Freedom Technique) Therapy against the decreased aggressiveness of adolescents fostered by Special Child Development Institutions (LPKA). *Jurnal Psikologi dan Psikologi Islam, 16*(1).

29. Prabowo, R. (2019). Efektivitas Terapi Spiritual Emotional Freedom Technique (SEFT). *Indonesian Journal of Health Development, 1*(2). Retrieved from https://ijhd.upnvj.ac.id/index.php/ijhd/article/view/17
30. Prabowo, R., Nurachmah, E., & Dahlia, D. (2019). Influence of Spiritual Emotional Freedom Technique (SEFT) on anxiety levels in congestive heart failure (CHF) patients. *Journal of Indra Husada Health, 6*(2), 8. doi:10.36973/jkih.v6i2.138
31. Rosyanti, L., Hadi, I., Tanra, J., Islam, A., Natzir, R., Nasrum, M., Idrus, F., & Bahar, B. (2019). Change of Brief Psychiatric Rating Scale (BPRS) Value with Spiritual Qur'anic Emotional Freedom Technique (SQEFT) therapy on mental disorder patient. *Indian Journal of Public Health Research and Development, 10,* 374. doi:10.5958/0976-5506.2019.00074.3
32. Sonhaji, S., & Lekatompessy, R. (2019) The effectiveness of Spiritual Emotional Freedom Technique (SEFT) and singing to elderly blood pressure at the Rumpelsos Pucang Gading Semarang. *Health Sciences and Pharmacy Journal, 3*(1), 14–20.
33. Susilowati, T., Pramana, N., & Muis, S. (2019). Non pharmacological interventions on anxiety in Primigravida. *Scientific Journal of Permas: Scientific Journal of STIKES Kendal, 9*(3), 181–186.
34. Warni, M., & Hayana, H. (2019). Description of the success of SEFT therapy in people with hypertension in Pandau Jaya Kec. Siak Hulu Kab. Kampar Village. *Photon: Journal of Science and Health, 10*(1), 24–30. doi:10.37859/jp.v10i1.1452
35. Wati, N., Mirayanti, N., & Juanamasta, G. (2019). The effect of Emotional Freedom Technique Therapy on nurse burnout. *JMMR (Jurnal Medicoeticolegal dan Manajemen Rumah Sakit), 8*(3),173–178. doi:10.18196/jmmr.83104
36. Afriyanti, E., & Wenni, B. (2018). The Effect of Spiritual Therapy Emotional Freedom Technique (SEFT) on the self-concept of breast cancer patients with mastectomy. *Jurnal Keperawatan Padjajaran (Padjadjaran Nursing Journal), 6*(3). doi:10.24198/jkp.v6i3.733
37. Hamidiyah, A., & Jannah, F. (2018). Intensity of primary dismenorhea pain before and after Spiritual Emotional Freedom Technique Therapy. *Oksitosin: Jurnal Ilmiah Kebidanan, 5*(1), 58–66. doi:10.35316/oksitosin.v5i1.361
38. Huda, S., & Alvita, G. (2018). The influence of SEFT therapy (Spiritual Emotional Freedom Technique) on reduction of blood pressure in hypertension patients in annual Puskemas area. *Journal of Nursing and Public Health, (Jurnal Keperawatan dan Kesehatan Masyarakat Cendekia Utama), 7*(2). doi:10.31596/jcu.v7i2.256
39. Kasron, K. (2018). Comparison of Spiritual Emotional Freedom Technique and progressive muscle relaxation on sleep quality of hypertension patients in South Cilacap. *Jurnal Kesehatan Poltekkes Kemenkes RI Pangkalpinang, 6*(1). doi:10.32922/jkp.v6i1.46
40. Khoeriyah, S., Lubis, D., Lubis, U., & Istichomah, I. (2018). Effect of Emotional Freedom Technique for emotional stability in adolescent prisoners. *Indonesian Nursing Journal of Education and Clinic, 3*(1), 15–21. doi:10.24990/injec.v3i1.169
41. Komang, N., Gandari, M., Ngurah, I., & Sentana, A. (2018). The Effect of Emotional Freedom Techniques therapy on learning concentration level of students. *Indonesian Journal of Health Research, 1*(2). doi:10.32805/ijhr.2018.1.2.12
42. Lismayanti, L. (2018). Effectiveness of Spiritual Emotional Freedom Therapy (SEFT) in reducing blood pressure in the elderly who have hypertension. *Proceedings of the National Seminar and Health Research, 1*(1).
43. Madoni, R., Wibowo, M., & Japar, M. (2018). Group counselling with systematic desensitization and Emotional Freedom Techniques to reduce public speaking anxiety. *Journal of Guidance for Counseling, 7*(1), 28–35. doi:10.15294/JUBK.V7I1.22679
44. Mardjan, M., Prabandari, Y., Hakimi, M., & Marchira, C. (2018). Emotional Freedom Techniques for reducing anxiety and cortisol level in pregnant adolescent primiparous. *Unnes Journal of Public Health, 7*(1), 1–6. doi:10.15294/ujph.v7i1.19212
45. Ma'rifah, A., Handayani, R. & Dewi, P. (2018). The effectiveness of fingerhold relaxation technique and Spiritual Emotional Freedom Technique (SEFT) on the pain intensity scale of patients with post Caesarean section. *Journal of Maternity Care and Reproductive Health, 1*(2). doi:10.36780/jmcrh.v1i2.28
46. Navianti, D., Garini, A., & Karneli, K. (2018). The reduction of anxiety and pain during venous blood sampling using Hypno-EFT (Emotional Freedom Techniques) method. *Public Health of Indonesia, 4*(2), 67–72. doi:10.36685/phi.v4i2.154
47. Novitriani, A., & Hidayati, F. (2018). The Spiritual Emotional Freedom Technique's influence on self-acceptance of inmates in women's penitentiaries. *Psympathic: Jurnal Ilmiah Psikologi, 5*(1), 1–12. doi:10.15575/psy.v5i1.2322
48. Patriyani, R., & Rahayu, S. (2018). The effect of Spiritual Emotional Freedom Technique (SEFT) on the reduction of blood sugar levels in diabetes in diabetes mellitus Type 2 in Rsud Kota Surakarta. *Journal of Health Sciences, 7*(2).
49. Puspita, E. (2018). Spiritual effects of Emotional Freedom Technique (SEFT) against decreased primary dysmenorrhea in young women. *Quality Journal of Health, 1*(1), 14–19.
50. Rosyanti, L., Hadi, I., Tanra, J., & Islam, A. (2018). The effectiveness of Spiritual Qur'anic Emotional Freedom Technique (SQEFT) intervention against the change of Brief Psychiatric Rating Scale (BPRS) on patients with schizophrenia. *Health Notions, 2*(8).
51. Sahlia, M., Wantiyah, W., & Hakam, N. (2018). The effect of Emotional Freedom Technique (EFT) therapy on depression in hypertensive clients. *Health Library, 6*(3), 446–452. Retrieved from https://jurnal.unej.ac.id/index.php/JPK/article/view/11687
52. Etika, A. N., Haryuni, S., & Sulistya, W. (2017). Difference in effectiveness between SEFT therapy (Spiritual Emotional Freedom Technique) and Keronkong music therapy for severity of depression in the elderly. *Jurnal Ilmiah Keperawatan, 12*(2).
53. Jhansi, S., Rajeswari, H., & Indira, S. (2017). Effectiveness of emotional freedom techniques on anxiety. *International Journal of Applied Research, 3*(3), 82–83. doi:10.13140/RG.2.2.14027.03360
54. Kartikasari, B., Handini, F., & Putri, M. (2017). Effect of Emotional Freedom Technique (EFT) on fulfilling sleep needs in the elderly. *Malang Nursing Journal, 2*(1), 18–21. doi:10.36916/jkm.v2i1.21

55. Kim, Y-H. (2017). A Case Study of Emotional Freedom Technique (EFT) Counseling for well-being. *Journal of the Korea Entertainment Industry Association, 11*(3), 223. doi:10.21184/jkeia.2017.04.11.3.223
56. Kusnanto, K., Pradanie, R., & Karima, I. (2017). Spiritual Emotional Freedom Technique (SEFT) on the quality of life of lung tuberculosis patients. *Jurnal Keperawatan Padjadjaran, 4*(3). doi:10.24198/jkp.v4i3.284
57. Lee, S., Jeong, B., Chae, H., & Lim, J. (2017). Emotional Freedom Techniques (EFT) for students' mental health: A systematic review. *Journal of Oriental Neuropsychiatry, 28*(3), 165–182. doi:10.7231/jon.2017.28.3.165
58. Liu, J., Yang, L., & Chen, J. (2017). Effect of emotional freedom technique on perceived stress, anxiety and depression in cancer patients: A preliminary experiment. *Modern Clinical Nursing, 16*(10), 34–38. doi:10.3969/j.issn.1671-8283.2017.10.008
59. Soto-Vásquez, M. R., & Alvarado-García, P. A. A. (2017). Efecto del extracto fluido de *Passiflora edulis* y técnicas de libertad emocional EFT en el tratamiento de la ansiedad ante los exámenes (Effect of fluid extract of *Passiflora edulis* and emotional freedom techniques EFT on test anxiety treatment). *Medicina Naturista, 11*(2), 85–90.
60. Sutiyarsih, E., & Sri, F. (2017). Effectiveness of Emotional Freedom Technique (EFT) against depression in the elderly. *Journal of Health Sciences, 6*(1).
61. Yuswinda, K. (2017). Evidence base practice SEFT (Spiritual Emotional Freedom Technique) therapy effect on preoperative patient anxiety. *Medica Hospitalia, 4*(2). doi:10.36408/mhjcm.v4i2.321
62. Faridah, V.N. (2016). Changes in spiritual perception and domain to blood pressure hypertension patients resulting from Spiritual Emotional Freedom Technique (SEFT). *Surya, 8*(1), 60–71.
63. Kim, H-K., Lee, Y-H., Koo, C-D., & Sik, Y-P. (2016). Effects of Emotional Freedom Technique (EFT) as a forest healing program on menopausal symptoms and quality of life in middle-aged women. *Korean Forest Recreation Society, 20*(3), 83–95.
64. Ningsih, S. F., Karim, D., & Sabrian, F. (2016). The effectiveness of Emotional Freedom Technique (EFT) therapy on the anxiety of patients with stage II and III breast cancer. *Online Journal of Nursing Science Study Program Students at Riau University, 2*(2), 1501–1509.
65. Sastra, L., & Sari, G. (2016). The influence of Emotional Freedom Technique (EFT) on the decrease of dismenorrhea pain in adolescents. *Research in Applied Science and Education, 8*(1), 34–39. doi:10.22216/jit.2014.v8i1.451
66. Wahyuliarmy, A. (2016). Effectiveness of SEFT (Spiritual Emotional Freedom Technique) on drug addiction syndrome in the elderly. *Jurnal Psikologi Islam, 31*(1). doi:10.18860/psi.v13i1.6409
67. Abdi, M., & Abolmaali, K. (2015). The effect of emotional freedom technique (EFT) therapy on the reduction of aggression in single mothers. *Applied Mathematics in Engineering, Management and Technology, 3*(2), 476–483.
68. Astuti, R., Yosep, I., & Susanti, R. D. (2015). Effect of spiritual intervention Emotional Freedom Technique toward decrease the level of depression housewives with HIV. *Jurnal Keperawatan Padjadjaran (Padjadjaran Nursing Journal), 3*(1).
69. Banerjee, P., Puri, A., & Luqman, N. (2015). Emotional Freedom Technique: An alternative therapy in destressing. *International Journal of Application or Innovation in Engineering and Management, 4*(9). ISSN 2319–4847.
70. Etika, A., & Wijaya, D. (2015). The influence of Spiritual Emotional Freedom Technique (SEFT) on smoking intensity in students. *Care: Jurnal Ilmiah Ilmu Kesehatan (Scientific Journal of Health Sciences), 3*(3), 12–18.
71. Ghamsari, M., & Lavasani, M. (2015). Effectiveness of Emotional Freedom Technique on pregnant women's perceived stress and resilience. *Journal of Education and Sociology, 6*(2).
72. Hermanwan, C., Sobarningsih, N., & Rahayu, Y. (2015). Use of Emotional Freedom Technique (EFT) to improve student learning outcomes. *Jurnal Analisa, 2*(1), 1–10.
73. Kartikodaru, P., Hartoyo, M., & Wulandari, M. (2015). The effect of Spiritual Emotional Freedom Technique (SEFT) on decrease on chemotherapy patients' anxiety. *Scientific Work of Stikes Telogorejo, 4.*
74. Putra, A. (2015). Spiritual Emotional Freedom Technique (SEFT) to reduce anxiety in parents when children are become sexual previous victims. *Jurnal Intervensi Psikologi, 7*(1).
75. Rofacky, H., & Aini, F. (2015). The effects of Spiritual Emotional Freedom Technique (SEFT) therapy on blood pressure in hypertension patients. *Jurnal Keperawatan Soedirman, 10*(1), 41–52.
76. Susanti, D. (2015). The effect of Spiritual Emotional Freedom Technique (SEFT) on reduction of blood pressure in hypertension patients in Puhkesmas Puhang Padang Working Area. Master's thesis, Universitas Andalas. http://repo.unand.ac.id/128
77. Wijaya, D. (2015). Effect of therapy spiritual emotional freedom technique (SEFT) changes on blood pressure in elderly with hypertension. *Journal of Nursing Care, 4*(5).
78. Desmaniarti, Z., & Avianti, N. (2014). Spiritual Emotional Freedom Technique (SEFT) decreasing stress in patients with cervical cancer. *Jurnal Ners, 9*(1), 91–96. doi:10.20473/jn.v9i1.3233
79. Latifah, L., & Ramawati, D. (2014). Emotional intervention of Emotional Freedom Technique to reduce post operation pain of Caesarian section. *Indonesian Nursing Journal of Education and Clinic, 1*(1), 53–60.
80. Lee, S-W., Lee, Y-J., Yoo, S-W., Lee, R-D., & Park, S-J. (2014). Case series of panic disorder patients treated with Oriental Medical treatments and EFT. *Journal of Oriental Neuropsychiatry, 25*(1), 13–28.
81. MacKinnon, L. (2014). Deactivating the buttons: Integrating radical exposure tapping within a family therapy framework. *Australian and New Zealand Journal of Family Therapy, 35*, 244–260.
82. Shari, W. W., Suryani, S., & Emaliyawati, E. (2014). Emotional Freedom Techniques and anxiety level of patients undergoing percutaneous coronary intervention. *Jurnal Keperawatan Padjadjaran (Padjadjaran Nursing Journal), 2*(3), 133–145. doi:10.24198/jkp.v2i3.83
83. Song, S-Y., Lee, J-H., Suh, J-W., Kwon, C-Y., & Kim, J-W. (2014). Qualitative analysis of the influence of an Emotion Freedom Techniques (EFT) group treatment program for Hwa-Byung (suppressed anger) patients. *Journal of Oriental Neuropsychiatry, 25*(1), 29–38. doi:10.7231/jon.2014.25.1.029

84. Alwan, N. S., & Nawajha, Z. E. (2013). The effectiveness of a training program based on Emotional Freedom Technique in upgrading feelings of happiness for diabetics in Gaza. *Research on Humanities and Social Sciences, 3*(18), 6–17.
85. Bakara, D., Ibrahim, K., & Sriati, A. (2013). Effects of Spiritual Emotional Freedom Technique on anxiety and depression, acute coronary syndrome. *Jurnal Keperawatan Padjadjaran, 1*(1). doi:10.24198/jkp.v1i1.51
86. Kim, S-Y., Yin, C-S., Choi, I-W., & Kim, J-W. (2013). Trends of meridian-based psychotherapy: Review of researches on Emotional Freedom Technique (EFT). *Journal of Oriental Neuropsychiatry, 24.* doi:10.7231/jon.2013.24.Spc1.089
87. Mariyati, L., & Habibah, N. (2013). SEFT (Spiritual Emotional Freedom Technique) therapy to reduce smoking tendency in early adolescents. *Psikologia Jurnal Psikologi, 2*(1). doi:10.21070/psikologia.v2i1.142
88. Safitri, R., & Sadif, R. (2013). Spiritual Emotional Freedom Technique (SEFT) to reduce depression for chronic renal failure patients are in Cilacap Hospital to undergo hemodialysis. *International Journal of Social Science and Humanity, 3*(3). doi:10.7763/IJSSH.2013.V3.249
89. Ulfa, E. (2013). Spiritual Emotional Freedom Technique intervention to reduce stress disorders after the Mount Merapi eruption trauma. *Journal of Educational, Health and Community Psychology, 2*(1). doi:10.12928/jehcp.v2i1.3743
90. Lee, J-H., Suh, H-U., Chung, S-Y., & Kim, J-W. (2011). A preliminary study for the evaluation of the effects of EFT for insomnia in the elderly. *Journal of Oriental Neuropsychiatry, 22*(4),101–109. doi:10.7231/JON.2011.22.4.101
91. Hakam, M., Yetti, K. Hariyati, T. (2009). Spiritual Emotional Freedom Technique (SEFT) intervention to reduce the pain of cancer patients. *Makara, Health, 13*(2), 95–99.

REVIEW ARTICLE

Building Ethical Mindfulness to Maximize Your Practice of EFT

Dorothea Hover-Kramer

Abstract

This article explores the ways that ethical mindfulness can enhance EFT practice by focusing on four distinct areas for increased awareness: (a) the current context of energy therapies as a whole within the larger picture of leading national health care disciplines; (b) the exceptional aspects of a new energy therapy, such as EFT, that require practitioner awareness beyond the usual considerations needed for cognitive therapies; (c) criteria for selection of clients most appropriate for EFT interventions such as client willingness, responsiveness, and ability to give feedback; and (d) the best risk management practices to avoid pitfalls in one's practice while enhancing safeguards and rapport.

Keywords: ethical mindfulness, client selection criteria, cautions for using EFT, risk management, energy medicine ethics

Dorothea Hover-Kramer, EdD, RN, DCEP, a pioneer in the field of energy medicine, died on January 15, 2013, a month after writing this article, which was originally published in *The Clinical EFT Handbook: A Definitive Resource for Practitioners, Scholars, Clinicians, and Researchers*, Vol. 2 (Energy Psychology Press, 2013). Cofounder and past president of the Association for Comprehensive Energy Psychology (ACEP), Hover-Kramer was also a founding elder of the Healing Touch movement and served on the leadership council of the American Holistic Nurses Association. She authored nine textbooks about energy therapies, including the award-winning ethics book *Creating Healing Relationships: Professional Standards for Energy Therapy Practitioners.*

Since EFT (Emotional Freedom Techniques) was first introduced several decades ago, practitioner acceptance for addressing a large range of client issues with EFT has made it one of the most widely known of the energy therapies. EFT's easy accessibility and effects of rapid change for clients, however, often disguise the depth and breadth of possible outcomes. In addition, as explored in this article, ethical mindfulness can greatly enhance EFT's effectiveness and maximize client learning.

My personal experience comes from more than 20 years of teaching energy modalities, in both Healing Touch and Energy Psychology certification programs, to people who are not licensed in a specific mental health discipline. Based on my learning from students, I offer the following perspectives to enhance practitioner mindfulness in utilizing the innately powerful tools of EFT:

- The public context of a new, innovative complementary modality such as EFT
- The exceptional aspects of energy modalities of which practitioners must be aware
- Criteria for selecting the clients most appropriate for EFT interventions
- Best risk management practices

We'll explore each of these themes to allow you as a practitioner to bring these ideas into your own way of offering EFT's person-centered, caring approaches to your clients. One might say that many of the considerations are simply good common sense; in fact, you may already have thought about many of these ideas. Nevertheless, reality proves that common sense is, after all, not so common unless acknowledged and reinforced. The price of a client relationship gone in the wrong direction is much too high, both for the individuals concerned, and also for the future of EFT practice as a whole.

I. The Public Context of the Innovative, Complementary Modality of EFT

Although many practitioners of EFT have met with public recognition, it is important to remember that this practice is only one of the approximately 50 approaches that fall under the broad category called "energy psychology" (EP). New protocols and methods are continually being developed by creative psychotherapists to address various forms of emotional distress with energetic means. Energy psychologies are a subset of a much larger popular and growing discipline named "energy medicine" (EM) which includes more than 250 training programs (Thomas, 2010, p. 6). Both EP and EM are sought out by the American public because complex client issues such as chronic pain, persistent stress reaction patterns, and the challenges of aging are not adequately addressed within the framework of current Western medical approaches.

Of course, conventional medical care is required for most people who seek out the large number of "complementary/alternative modalities" as identified and accepted by the National Institutes of Health (NIH). As new methods are being researched, they begin to be recognized as "probably efficacious" by the large organizations of conventional medical and psychiatric practitioners, the purveyors of so-called "mainstream medicine." Energy medicine, also dubbed "frontier medicine," is the last item on NIH's long list of innovative modalities, such as herbal medicine, vitamin therapy, massage, and homeopathic practice, among others, that are currently being researched for future acceptance. It's valuable to recall that acupuncture, despite its 5,000-year history of providing pain relief, was only approved by the American Medical Association in the last decade for a specific number of applications. In November 2012, after a 12-year battle led by the Association for Comprehensive Energy Psychology (ACEP), the American Psychological Association (APA) approved energy psychology courses as acceptable material for psychologists' continuing education credits. APA still considers all energy therapies to be "experimental, and probably efficacious" despite the large, growing body of EP research (ACEP, 2012).

The bottom line is that energy medicine, energy psychology, and EFT specifically are still a long way from being a standard part of the nation's health care picture. The required cautions for practitioners are therefore to use the work wisely, with carefully selected clients, and always to ensure client informed consent.

Clients always have the right to choose whether to receive EFT or not, regardless of the practitioner's wish for good outcomes. They are not at fault if the results practitioners wish for them are not achieved. Other methods may actually be more effective for individual client issues. Networking, referral-making, and expanding practitioner resources are essential elements of all professional EFT practice.

Another aspect of client informed consent is for practitioners to educate clients about EFT clearly before beginning their work. This includes stating the possible benefits and risks of the innovative, experimental EFT treatment they will receive. Benefits are by now well known, but several of the benefits also have inherent client risks. For example, the rapid change induced by EFT can affect the client's family or occupational systems. If, for example, a low-key family member recalls her inner strengths and becomes effectively assertive, the whole family system will be affected, with reverberations to all family members.

Another benefit/risk now well documented is that clients' memories change. While this appears an adaptive change for the better in most cases, it could limit testimony in legal settings. The client and his or her environment must steadily be considered as client/practitioner agreements are made within a mutually set therapeutic contract.

II. Exceptional Aspects of EFT Requiring Practitioner Awareness

Unlike most cognitive, conversational therapies, EFT communicates on an energetic level. Far more than words is involved in the interaction between client and practitioner energy fields. The very presence of the practitioner can evoke hope and new possibilities if the caregiver is "walking his talk"—a living example of self-care and balanced mental, emotional, and spiritual energy. Every communication is sensed by both participants within the sacred, caring contract to reach the whole person. It is an art to communicate this degree of presence to others, and caregivers, especially in energy modalities, are mandated to engage in regular, daily self-care. (For further discussion of self-care, see Hover-Kramer, 2011, pp. 63–110.)

Another safeguard is to know your scope of practice. Specifically, what are your skills, background, and strengths as well as the areas in which you have limited or no expertise? Keeping a growing self-inventory allows insights to come from each client session. (For further discussion of scope of practice considerations, see Hover-Kramer, 2011, pp. 93–96, 139, 142–147.)

In addition to creating the setting for multidimensional healing to take place, practitioners are charged with recognizing their own perceptual limitations so they do not pass them on to their clients. Practitioner attachment to a specific outcome with the use of only one method such as EFT may be one of the most prominent of such projections. There are also, however, the clients' tendencies of wanting to please their helpers by agreeing too readily, not choosing what they need carefully, or becoming overly dependent. There is a real power differential, whether acknowledged or hidden, and all practitioners need to take it into account in obtaining informed consent and building the trusted healing relationship.

Because of the rapid and deeper rapport that occurs in energy therapies, clients may have increased and unrealistic emotional attachments to their practitioners. Client expectations may well exceed anything that can be offered. This is why mutual agreements around treatment goals are so vital at the outset. In addition, I encourage taking the last 10 minutes of every session to ask clients to tell you what they learned, how their view of themselves is changing, and to discuss what was helpful and what was not.

In addition to rapid rapport and the opportunity for full dimensional healing, another unusual feature of energy therapies is the possible presence of varying degrees of trance. The repetition of phrases combined with stimulation of acupoints readily brings clients to deeper awareness of themselves, which may include nonordinary states of consciousness. On a continuum, these may range from mild trance or reverie, to reliving a traumatic event, stepping into a childhood memory, or recalling a period of human history, or moving to a sense of transcending the present, experiencing a sense of spiritual Oneness. Since all these possibilities are healthy signs of human functioning, practitioners must be prepared to normalize these experiences. Validating and honoring clients' unusual responses helps clients accept and integrate whatever material surfaces from the rich treasures of their unconscious minds. The intention of the psyche in opening doors to new awareness is always positive, toward growth and increased wisdom.

Another exceptional feature of energy therapies is that archetypal patterns are often much more active and conscious than in talk therapies. Archetypes are elemental individual and relationship patterns that have been repeated throughout human history. One of the most readily understood is the Parent/Child archetype. As the therapeutic relationship develops, the Child archetype may become activated in a needy client; the helper may respond by temporarily comforting or parenting the client. If the Parent archetype becomes activated more extensively by giving advice or direction, however, the client can slip into dependency on the practitioner in ways that hamper positive outcomes in areas such as personal decision-making, individuating, or becoming more assertive. Other possible archetypes that can be seen in many therapeutic relationships are the Master/Slave or Helper/Victim patterns. Some caregivers may also think they are evoking the Healer archetype when they are actually living from Servant or Martyr archetypal patterns.

Practitioner mindfulness is thus essential in handling rapid rapport, the closeness of biofield interactions, the likelihood of nonordinary states of consciousness, and the possibility of falling into archetypal patterns—all of which can occur in energetic interventions. These cautions exist for EFT practitioners *in addition* to the usual safeguards and practitioner guidelines emphasized in the standard ethics courses for licensed mental health practitioners. (For a summary of standard ethical guidelines in licensed mental health practices, see Hover-Kramer, 2011, pp. 124–125.)

III. Criteria for Selecting Clients Who Can Most Benefit from EFT

Careful assessments of clients before beginning EFT work with them is essential in avoiding possible later dilemmas. Some clients seek out energy therapies to avoid receiving conventional medical care; others have simply heard about EFT and want to try it for themselves; and some who have experienced many treatment failures in other settings may seek you out as their "last hope." Whatever the motivation, it's helpful to know what brings clients your way before contracting to work together or developing a treatment plan.

Remember that you are not the only resource or "last hope" for anyone; there are plenty of referral or consultation resources available via the Internet to connect practitioners and specialists in all time zones. Some clients may benefit from having a good medical evaluation first because early symptoms of many illnesses such as cancer or diabetes can show up as depression, nightmares, or negative thinking patterns. Others may benefit from learning self-care practices to manage their emotional distress long before you introduce tapping or another EFT intervention.

The kinds of clients who can make the best progress with a good, basic knowledge of EFT and your self-insights as a practitioner are those who: are interested in the work, have well-defined issues such as a recent trauma or anxiety, are willing to make mutual agreements to work with you, and are willing to participate in their personal growth through homework and giving feedback.

These parameters then remind us of the personality patterns that may hamper reaching positive outcomes: lack of interest in EFT or personal development, suspiciousness, feeling scattered, becoming easily confused or distracted, having poor recall, holding unrealistic expectations, being unwilling to engage in treatment planning or follow suggestions, and having severe physical issues or allergies or enmeshed, complex problems. Although some of these individuals may be helped by some of what EFT can offer, they may actually do much better, more rapidly with more intensive in-depth psychological or medical work that fits your personal scope of practice or inclinations.

Matching client needs to the best possible treatment is an essential skill for EFT practitioners, as many do not have long-term study in mental health or social sciences. Of course, given our world of natural and political disasters, human suffering continues to be extensive. There are many, many relatively healthy people who can benefit greatly from the accessibility and effectiveness of EFT without needing more in-depth, long-term interventions. Mindful, ethical EFT practitioners know their strengths and limitations in selecting the clients that can most benefit from what they have to offer.

IV. Best Risk-Management Practices

To summarize and embellish on the previous considerations, here are some of the most effective and elegant ways to maximize building healing relationships with your clients:

- Make sure every bit of publicity, including websites and email signatures, about you is accurate. This includes your credentials, educational background, interests, years of practice, and strengths.
- Make realistic and proven statements about the method you're using. Avoid making unfounded claims about EFT. Although many positive outcomes have been noted, neither EFT nor any other energy-oriented method can totally cure illness, prevent disease, or answer every problem.
- Keep backup materials of EFT theory and research so you can readily answer client or public questions. Enhance your library and knowledge base regularly.
- Carefully document initial informed consent about using EFT with clients and thereafter "check in" regularly with clients with every intervention you offer. Ask for permissions respecting client wishes; keep confidentiality except in cases where the client's or another person's life is at high risk.
- Ensure that all clients have recent and adequate medical evaluation and care as needed.
- Develop a wide and experienced referral network. Make clients aware that you may consider referral to more expert practitioners or leaders from other disciplines as needed.
- Utilize consultation on a regular basis. No one person can anticipate the challenges you may encounter, but always know you are not alone.
- Be proactive in noting signs of reduced or missing client rapport and ask frequently for feedback.
- Know your scope of practice, your personal strengths and weaknesses, and also what kinds of practice are legally permitted in your community.
- Set goals together with your clients and hold them to the boundaries you establish regarding visits, telephone calls, emails, fees, and so on.
- Hold the stance of "facilitating being led" by your clients. They know the truth about who they are; it is not your place to guess or assume you know what they need.

- Avoid dual or complex relationships such as seeing several members of one family unless there are clear, up-front agreements to do so.

Though no one can guarantee success in all endeavors because clients can come from widely divergent experiences, these considerations will go a long way toward helping you maximize your effectiveness and minimize unhappy experiences. EFT practice allows you to share your intention of goodwill with skill and inner wisdom in a world of need. Mindful, ethical practice is the heart of EFT in action!

References

Association for Comprehensive Energy Psychology (ACEP). (2012). *APA approves ACEP to provide CE credits for psychologists.* Retrieved from http://energypsych.org/displaycommon.cfm?an=1&subarticlenbr=329

Hover-Kramer, D. (2011). *Creating healing relationships: Professional standards for energy therapy practitioners.* Santa Rosa, CA: Energy Psychology Press.

Thomas, L. (2010). *The encyclopedia of energy medicine.* Minneapolis, MN: Fairview Press.

If you would like to write book reviews for Energy Psychology *journal, we'd love to hear from you. Get inspiring books for free! Contact Stephanie Marohn at angel@stephaniemarohn.com*

Making the Case for EFT and Energy Psychology: Designing, Conducting and Publishing Case Studies

Elizabeth Boath, PhD

Amazon Kindle, 2021
158 pages (print version)
$9.99
ISBNs:
978-1739708009 English e-version
978-1739708016 English Paperback
978-1739708023 Dutch e-version
978-1739708030 Dutch Paperback
978-1739708047 Spanish e-version
978-1739708054 Spanish Paperback

Reviewed by Peta Stapleton

As a research academic and EFT trainer and practitioner, I truly wish this book had been available when I started out. Professor Boath has provided a practical and comprehensive blueprint for EFT and Energy Psychology (EP) clinicians to document client outcomes effectively and consistently and share them in a professional manner. The medical field has long used single case studies to demonstrate unique differences between patients and possible methodologies to be tested in larger trials. The EP and EFT world needs to take advantage of this model as well.

Making the Case for EFT and Energy Psychology not only presents the rationale for practitioners to pursue single case study publications but also shows how non-academic therapists can read existing research and evaluate single case studies. (The book has been translated into Spanish and Dutch as well.) Especially due to the chapter on how to search for studies and how to evaluate them, I truly wish this book had been available decades ago!

Professor Boath also provides a comprehensive list of freely available outcome tools to help clinicians evaluate client change and progress, and defines why this is vital for effective therapeutic work. The inevitable hurdle many therapists face is getting clients to complete homework, and Professor Boath addresses ways to do this. Should practitioners wish to publish their client outcomes and, having reached this section in the book, they will be well equipped to do so. Topics such as client consent (example forms are included in the book) and ethical review processes and guidelines to follow are clearly presented. Even those unattached to university settings will learn how to have their client case studies reviewed by external bodies.

Making the Case for EFT and Energy Psychology is clear in the process of writing a case study for review and professional publication. While reading chapter 3, I even learnt some incredibly useful hacks for referencing! Suitable journal examples are supplied along with how to access these and an overview of the submission process. Should practitioners wish to pursue these types of publications in a group rather than as a solo venture, Professor Boath also provides a way to do this (by developing a case study cluster).

Despite government funding, exceptionally high-quality clinical trials, and outstanding outcomes, even the best research may never be read. To combat this issue, *Making the Case for EFT and Energy Psychology* offers readers a way to disseminate and share their published case studies in innovative ways.

Part of the battle may be actual publication, but the next vital step is sharing it. Chapter 9 presents a clear process and some creative ways to do this.

This book is essential reading. Every EFT and EP practitioner will gain something beneficial for their client work and practice, even if publishing case studies is not their passion. The chapters on assessing client outcomes are worth the purchase price alone, and I will definitely be recommending it to all my students to read!

Should you be interested in sharing the unique and effective outcomes your clients are achieving, this is the book for you. What can be a daunting process is made clear and concise in this book. Publishing case studies will also instill confidence in EFT and EP practitioners, which trainings alone do not offer. I believe this book should be mandatory in EFT and EP trainings.

Everyone should read this book. Do yourself a favor and buy a copy now.

Peta Stapleton, PhD, is a researcher, author, EFT practitioner and trainer, and associate professor in the School of Psychology at Bond University in Queensland, Australia. Email: pstaplet@bond.edu.au

From Triggered to Tranquil: How Self-Compassion and Mindful Presence Can Transform Relationship Conflicts and Heal Childhood Wounds

Susan Campbell

New World Library, 2021
Softcover, 248 pages
$16.95
ISBN: 978-1608687404

Reviewed by Carol A. Atkinson

Book titles are intended to trigger a need in a potential reader. This book's title, *From Triggered to Tranquil*, certainly does that. All of us have people in our lives who tend to trigger our anger and fear, and the lid of the blame game can easily pop open. The journey through Susan Campbell's book can in itself trigger considerable feelings. She is a master at knowing just the right question to reveal one's own emotional land mines.

It is the last chapter, though, that brings the book its deepest application. Chapter 12, titled "I'm Triggered by the World Situation," provides a profound opportunity to use Campbell's method at a macro level, which few methods or authors actually offer. How does a person become tranquil as one explores childhood wounds and relationship conflicts in relation to the national and international aggression in the past many years? That is the gem in this book, albeit it hidden on page 215.

Campbell writes:

> "The more stressed out we feel, the more triggerable we are. And the more easily we can be manipulated by special interest groups who seek to hijack our amygdala or take advantage of our dysregulated state to push their agendas. If we want to maintain a sense of equanimity and inner sovereignty in this chaotic world, we need good self-regulation." (p. 216)

Indeed, self-regulation is the core of this method. Campbell teaches how to stop once triggered, pause and calm down, attempt to discover the core wounding, and finally repair the upset with the other person. She suggests remembering that the feelings of hurt or fear that arose during an emotional event are not really feelings but "projections of your core fears onto another's behavior" (p. 55). The method is a five-step process that can begin the healing of core emotional issues (p. 16):

- Admit and accept your insecurities
- Learn your unique trigger signature
- Pause to regulate yourself
- Be with the emotions and sensations
- Repair and clear the air

These steps, as introduced in chapter 1, are flushed out in each of the succeeding chapters in Part I. There, Campbell explores in depth the science and the method in each of the five steps. More critically, in each chapter, Campbell provides meditations and deeply probing questions to trigger the reader's own buried issues.

Admitting our insecurities takes considerable self-awareness and wholeness. But this process is all about self-discovery. By being strong in stopping a confrontation or flight and reviewing the event in a calm and self-parenting environment, a person can discover the core fear or wounding. When one is triggered, Campbell suggests pausing, regulating one's own emotions by just accepting and witnessing the ways in which emotions can flow. In that time of self-discovery, a trigger signature (or how a person is most often triggered) can be developed. This is a key part of the process: noticing behavioral patterns and using them as a way to understand that what seems to be at issue isn't the issue.

In Part II, Campbell explores examples of triggering events, whether from one's children, partner, or colleague or a national or international issue. For example, she tells the story of a Mexican-American client who was so overwhelmed by the political communication occurring in the nation that she couldn't watch television or read the news. Campbell walked the client through the five-step process to understand how the contemporary political situation mirrored her own growing up as a minority in a white world. Her sense of worthlessness, abuse, and attack were all mirrored in contemporary culture. Once the client moved through the process, she was able to stand up for those being abused and to step into developing support programming for the minority community.

Frankly, none of this method seems particularly easy. In fact, doing this work by oneself takes time, enormous patience, and compassionate self-assessment. The primary component of the method is self-calming and self-soothing, which even on the best of days is not always easy. However, it would seem that, once learned, this method could be incredibly rewarding: moving from triggered to accepting responsibility for the confrontation is a step to self-actualization. From a practitioner's point of view, this method is an immensely helpful processes that can be used in sum or in parts to help a client see through their emotional issues.

Campbell's book is written with great clarity and ease. For that alone, the book is well worth reading. For those who are truly on the path to healing the emotional body, this book is a very important one.

Carol Atkinson, PhD, is a professor of digital media specializing in free speech, gender in the media, and personal interests in the myriad levels of consciousness. Email: atkinson@ucmo.edu

Extraordinary Awakenings: When Trauma Leads to Transformation

Steve Taylor, PhD
New World Library, 2021
Softcover, 264 pages
$18.95 US
ISBN: 978-1608687671

Reviewed by Steve Manire

In the 1960s, Dionne Warwick sang, "What the world needs now is love, sweet love." It will likely take an extraordinary awakening to bring that about in today's world.

In his book *Extraordinary Awakenings*, Steve Taylor expresses a possibility, and a hope, that such extraordinary awakenings may be part of an evolutionary process through which humankind may be shifting into a higher-functioning, awakened state. As a senior lecturer in psychology at Leeds Beckett University, chair of the Transpersonal Psychology Section of the British Psychological Society, and author of numerous other books on psychology and spirituality, Dr. Taylor has extensive knowledge of his subject.

In this book, he tells the stories of some of the many people who have experienced life-changing awakenings, most of them sudden, in various traumatic situations: prison, war, medical conditions, bereavement, addictions, near suicides. He coined the term "transformation through turmoil" (TTT) to describe what these "shifters," as he calls them, have undergone: life-changing awakening through extreme suffering.

While the shifters' lives do not suddenly become perfect, their lives are suddenly and permanently based on an entirely new awareness of life that is profoundly spiritual, though not generally religious, and difficult to convey to other people. Dr. Taylor states: "Everyone who experiences TTT discovers that what we think of as normal is an aberrational state that creates psychological suffering and presents us with a false vision of reality. Awakening gives us access to a fuller, higher-functioning state in which life seems easy and we feel at home in the world."

The shifters may, however, require a significant period, sometimes years, to understand and adapt to this new, all-encompassing awareness of life, at least as it relates to living in the circumstances of their lives prior to awakening.

Chapter by chapter, Dr. Taylor tells the shifters' stories and the traumas that led to their awakenings.

In chapter 1, "Peace in the Midst of War," we learn about Gus who, in the Falkland Islands war, accepted the prospect of death and suddenly "there was peace. Complete peace … Time disappeared, and I was filled with ecstasy … I was completely reconciled to whatever happened." The stories of others in this chapter further express the extraordinary awakenings related to wartime suffering. Dr. Taylor believes there may be as many as millions of soldiers who have had similar experiences over the thousands of years that wars have been fought.

In chapters 2 and 3, "Freedom in Prison," Taylor posits that incarceration may have the highest degree of spiritual potential. Prisoners' confinement to a single room with limited space, loss of autonomy, and other privations is compared to the "voluntary incarceration" of some monks and nuns, with obvious differences noted. Both involve extreme detachment and a great deal of solitude and inactivity. For a small number of prisoners, this may have a positive spiritual effect. A story that most impressed this reviewer was that of Ananta Kranti, whose awakening in a brutal Japanese prison (she is British) enabled her to feel "pure compassion" for the brutal guards, "no matter how badly they treated us" because she was "able to see the guards as the real prisoners." After her release, she went through a very challenging phase of adjustment and integration as she explored how to live in this world as an awakened person, how to "walk this earth as divine human beings." The story of Ed Little, a 56-year-old man in an Arkansas prison since age 16, is equally moving, as he shifted from the emotionally frozen young boy to a man who could experience empathy for another's pain or joy.

Chapter 4, "Transformation through Bereavement," notes that acceptance is an important factor in TTT and bereavement is a major trigger in transformation, though understandably many find the death of a loved one difficult to accept. In his own research, Dr. Taylor found that his research participants' transformational experiences resulted in numerous positive changes for nearly all of them. These changes were common characteristics of wakefulness, shared by all of the shifters in this book.

The stories cited in chapter 5, "Transformation through Facing Death," involve being diagnosed with terminal illness (what Dr. Taylor terms an "intense mortality experience" or IME) or having a near-death experience (NDE). This reviewer appreciated that Dr. Taylor, while putting forth his ideas about the shifters' experiences, discusses them with a balance of respect for the shifter's experience and pursuance of the researcher's desire to understand and seek truth. Of note: At some point we all are going to have an intense mortality experience, and evidence suggests that this encounter will be transformational for most of us.

Chapter 6, "On the Brink of Suicide," discusses transformation through depression and stress. Dr. Taylor notes the many causes of depression, suggesting that most depression is strongly related to environmental and existential factors rather than neurological ones, and even cites spiritual repression as a potential cause (which he experienced as a younger man). This chapter considers three cases of TTT triggered by long periods of intense depression. One person actually experienced his awakening via a vivid dream while he was asleep, becoming aware of significant changes when he woke up and was clearly a different person, who now knew that his "true 'me' is just awareness itself."

The amazing result of the awakenings in chapter 7, "Release from Craving," is the immediate and total release from addiction, as though "the old self that was burdened with the addiction dies, and a new self takes its place." Dr. Taylor emphasizes here that "spiritual awakening is not the end of the journey, but the beginning of a different journey, often a challenging process of adjustment and integration, requiring self-understanding and self-acceptance."

In chapter 8, "Explaining Transformation Through Turmoil," Dr. Taylor, loving the idea that some phenomena are simply mysterious or magical and there's no point trying to explain them, nevertheless offers his possible explanations for transformation through turmoil. I will not spoil your future reading of the book by attempting to summarize his explanations! He even considers the question "Why doesn't TTT happen to everyone?" and notes that the factors in play here may be a certain personality type (hint: transliminal mind) and one's attitude about the psychological turmoil (hint: acceptance), among others. Is TTT just self-delusion? He welcomes healthy skepticism, but is wary of "humbugism." (The appendix highlights 18 major characteristics of wakefulness in four areas: perceptual, affective, conceptual/cognitive, and behavioral.)

In chapter 9, Learning from Transformation Through Turmoil," Dr. Taylor considers two main learnings gleaned from the shifters' experiences: how to respond to suffering and turmoil in our lives, and some basic principles we can apply in our own spiritual development. He offers methods and techniques he has developed from what he has learned. He does not suggest that we should welcome suffering or purposely seek it out (self-flagellation is so medieval), but simply being aware that suffering can have some positive effects may be beneficial, may have something to teach us.

In the book's conclusion, "The Most Extraordinary Awakening," Dr. Taylor maintains that it is impossible to separate spiritual awakening from the evolution of consciousness. When shifters undergo awakening, it represents an evolutionary progression to a higher self. He notes that in every single case of TTT, it is the same higher self that emerges, representing an unfolding and revealing of an already established structure. He posits that the higher-functioning state of the shifters "may be lying in wait for all human beings." Recalling that the problems created in our "sleep state" cannot be solved from that same state, Dr. Taylor offers that we need to wake up to survive! Will we do it? Will we wake up in time to avert major disasters? He believes that consciously cultivating spiritual awakening individually can contribute to the collective awakening of our species.

"And that will be the most extraordinary awakening of all."

Steve Manire was a practicing chiropractor for 30 years and an EFT practitioner with the Vet Stress Project. He is well-loved by his two awakened dogs, Harvey and Silvie. Email: steve.manire@gmail.com

Beyond Medicine: A Physician's Revolutionary Prescription for Achieving Absolute Health and Finding Inner Peace

Patricia A. Muehsam, MD

New World Library, 2021
Softcover, 304 pages
$17.95
ISBN: 978-1608686995

Reviewed by Lorna Minewiser

Beyond Medicine is a fascinating read as well as a prescription for what Dr. Muehsam calls "Absolute Health." It is filled with personal vignettes, exercises, and a brief history of alternative medicine, consciousness, and manifestation as well as her experiences with extraordinary healers. Throughout she reminds the reader, "You are the Medicine." An internal medicine physician, she was a pioneer in teaching alternative medicine, served on the Mind Body Interventions panel of the newly established NIH Office of Alternative Medicine, and has been a researcher in the field.

Today she practices "Transformational Medicine" and her book *Beyond Medicine* teaches how to access our "inner healer." She describes the "Five Absolute Health Tools" that help us do this, as well as the "Four Primary Medicines." In each of the chapters that follow and with downloadable audio recordings, she demonstrates with appropriate exercises how to use the "absolute health tools."

The Four Primary Medicines are food, lifestyle, relationships/community, and purpose. Her prescriptions in these areas are not one-size-fits-all but are uniquely tailored to each person. In an exercise on how to make lifestyle your medicine, she says: "Moment-to-moment awareness. Being present. Being here now, checking within, listening to what your body and mind need" (p. 54). This advice is echoed throughout the book.

The Five Tools for Absolute Health are breathwork, journaling, mindfulness and meditation, mirror work, and mind-body sensing. In each chapter, she suggests several exercises for addressing the topic of the chapter. She most often includes breathing exercises, some of which are useful at any time, not only on topic. In the chapter on mind-body sensing, she includes energy medicine and Emotional Freedom Techniques (EFT).

> "EFT can be used for any and all health concerns and issues, whether we are dealing with a physical issue or difficult emotions .... [it's] a potent practice for shifting circumstances and situations that feel challenging .... EFT helps the mind and body return to a place of balance." (p. 75)

Dr. Muehsam describes a number of other healing practices, including Ayurveda, homeopathy, traditional Chinese medicine, and bodywork and body-centered practices. An appendix offers an extensive reference for books, practitioners, and websites.

Throughout the book, Dr. Muehsam reminds us of the importance of feeling our feelings, and there are exercises to help us learn how to do that. While there are chapters on consciousness, manifestation, and miracles, she reminds us to experiment with the Absolute Health Tools and find our way to the "Inner Healer" that resides in each of us, because, as she reiterates, "You are the Medicine" (p. 234).

I found this to be a fascinating read and highly recommend it to anyone who wants to take charge of their own health.

Lorna Minewiser, PhD, is a retired Licensed Professional Counselor, ACEP Certified Energy Health Practitioner, and master EFT trainer. She was part of the Veterans Stress Project, helping veterans with PTSD, and has written several articles for peer-reviewed journals. Email: Lorna@coachminewiser.com

Letting Go of Nothing: Relax Your Mind and Discover the Wonder of Your True Nature

Peter Russell
New World Library, 2021
Hardcover, 152 pages
$17.95
ISBN: 978-1608687657

Reviewed by Dawn O'Creene

I must admit that I squeezed reading *Letting Go of Nothing* into my chaotic schedule. I was in the middle of being in a theater production, being part of an amicable relationship breakup (due to different future wants), two paying jobs, one volunteer job (the Zen of my week—feeding raptors), and did I mention a move?

This book was tailor-made for such a time. While we thought that Covid perhaps gave us a small taste of slowing down, it seems the Busy Bug has hit harder than ever. As this is an Eckhart Tolle edition book, it was chosen by the No Fuss King himself as a work of excellence for helping others find some peace in their busy lives.

Filled with bite-sized, manageable chapters that can be read in any order, Peter Russell imparts realistic inspiration. You don't have to be monastic about pursuing spiritual practice. You just get to be wonderful, imperfect you. I was thrilled finally to find permission to enjoy sensory pleasures, and even possessions (to a healthy degree, of course), alongside pursuing a spiritual path. Can this be for real? Absolutely. The catch? Enjoy the pleasures while they last rather than seek them out, says Russell. Allow them to be in your moment without these sensations or objects having addictive qualities.

We've all heard many times the phrase "letting go," but what does it mean? According to Russell, it means letting go of the grasp we have on things. It's freeing to treat moments as you would an old-fashioned mixer ball. You enjoy the dance in each moment with each person, knowing you will let go to change partners and switch to another mental environment. And another. And another. The grasp is stressful, says Russell. Holding on to things from worry they will go away brings in fear, no matter how small the level. He urges us to imagine no longer grasping. We expend energy holding on to things that don't serve us. Grasping holds hands with suffering.

Russell applies grasping to ideas, emotions, physical possessions, ego, our personal stories, discontent, and relationships, exploring how to apply letting go to each of them. The benefits of letting go await you, he says. Letting go nourishes curiosity, creativity, and new ways of thinking and being. What's awaiting you in your future … what if? The new way involves letting ideas in without pushing them away and then allowing them to formulate in your consciousness for exploration, and letting go of fear or "This is the way I've always done it."

Sometimes distraction is a strategy we use to avoid distress. We live in a society where distraction is the norm in so many ways. But if we are using distraction to avoid emotional pain, we are missing something important, warns Russell. He reminds us that pain is *meant* to draw attention. It yells, "Over here! Fix me please! Something is amiss!" We can't relieve ourselves of emotional pain without attending to it, spending the time to learn what it wants. Letting go in this case, according to Russell, is using strength not in holding the door shut to what we fear, but in taking a deep breath and letting the door open to show us what is on the other side.

Letting Go of Nothing is loaded with gems. Russell effortlessly puts forth complicated ideas that can be easily assimilated as if they are rudimentary. He writes of "Returning to the Natural Mind," which is a state of no fears or wants, when all is "simply okay."

If all humans could attain that state, the world would be a much more civil and happier place. "Simply okay" means your needs are met. You are not hot, cold, or hungry. You are not in pain, tired, or sad. In this moment, you have everything you need. Russell highlights that need, want, and fear flip okayness to discontent. Discontent arises for many of us, however, even when we have all we need.

Letting go involves examining and adjusting our relationships with fear, obsessiveness, worry, grudges, and grievances, and being at home with being imperfect, to name a few areas. Too often we notice the discomforts of our lives instead of savoring the moment. Chances are if you are reading this right now, you are in a comfortable state. You're not drifting away on an Arctic ice floe, ducking a bullet, being sought by a python in the jungle, or watching your home flood. Russell calls on us to take this moment to savor our good fortune and acknowledge that we are indeed blessed in ways that others may not be.

Peter Russell helps us understand the many ways we hold ourselves back from simple happiness, but he doesn't just deposit us there. He helps us also understand how to move beyond this, which reminds me of the following parable.

When an elephant is young, a trainer puts a sizable rope around his leg and ties him to something he can't break away from. The elephant learns that no matter how he tries, he can't get away. Eventually, the rope can be tied to the elephant's leg without being tethered to anything else and yet the elephant doesn't leave. His mind has accepted that if the rope is tied to his leg, he can't run free.

We too imprison ourselves inside the box of our minds as a result of previous negative experiences or thoughts passed down to us by others. Letting go of prior limited thinking while allowing curiosity, healthy experimentation, and alternative paths can be just what we need to find our "simply okay."

Dawn O'Creene works as a finance analyst by day and enjoys being a library clerk by night. You can find her on the stage of her community theater when she is not working behind the scenes. She believes you can never stop learning or have too many books. Email: gazingraven@gmail.com

Becoming an Empowered Empath: How to Clear Energy, Set Boundaries, and Embody Your Intuition

Wendy De Rosa
New World Library, 2021
Softcover, 208 pages
$15.95
ISBN: 978-1608687190

Reviewed by Carol A. Atkinson

Much of medical science and many counselors, healers, and self-help authors seek to eliminate human pain, numbing it, altering it, or preventing the mind from noticing it. Wendy De Rosa intends to help empathic people (empaths) who feel pain acutely. The pain is often that of other people, perhaps of the events and changes going on throughout the planet, and even of the degradation of nature. "Empaths experience their world through their intuition and a felt sense of people and situations. They may not be able to define why they feel the way they do, but they sense that they are impacted by other people's energy" (p. 1). More importantly, and more unusually, De Rosa insists that empaths do not have to manage energy as they learned to do to compensate for their sensitivities, but "instead they are here to raise consciousness, leading by example with true sensitivity and heart" (p. 5).

In this powerful and distinctly loving book, De Rosa writes that empaths listen attentively and are usually loved for that gift, but all too often that attention turns into taking on another's feelings and experiences as if it is happening to the empath. A variety of body problems can result: irritation, fatigue, pain, troubled thoughts, or the mirror of the pain of the other person. De Rosa says this is caused by empaths not being fully in their energy bodies, specifically ungrounded in their lower chakras, leaving a vacancy for others to take over.

Counselors and practitioners are all familiar with those who lived in dysfunctional families and within them was a child who had to create some peace and love in the experience. The child was usually attempting to create a safe environment by being intimately aware of others' moods and inclinations; she notes that such children usually decide to take on the chaotic energy to manage it rather than be overwhelmed by it.

> "These survival and coping mechanisms take root in the first chakra area of the body and, once formed, create energetic imprints in your body that can lead to unhealthy [relationship] patterns .... Largely unconscious, this response becomes ingrained as a default setting, influencing your worldview and how you interact." (p. 3)

These are deep and enduring energetic patterns that De Rosa seeks to repair: restoring energetic boundaries and allowing the empath's true self to emerge. She advocates journaling as a means of processing root chakra imprints. Thus, in each chapter, she reviews the substance of her teaching and then provides prompts for journaling. Once that is accomplished to completion, she recommends and offers a meditation. Fortunately, the reader can visit her website for the electronic version of the meditation rather than relying on memory or reading.

In chapter 1, De Rosa sets readers on the path of clarity, asking them to set an intention for what they want out of the book by focusing on their heart. "Through the heart chakra, your Soul is calling you to live in alignment with your gifts. Listen deeply with the light of your heart. What is it asking of you in this life?" (p. 7). Then she asks you to clarify what you want most to create in your life and what patterns you seek to release.

She asks readers to revisit their family of origin and look at what their role in it was and how were they made to feel. She writes that empaths should thank their disassociation, the flight-or-flight response, the pattern of overeating (p. 24) for saving them, but they need all of that to go away now. Grounding is the first step to building a new way of being. A chapter is dedicated to doing that, through journaling and meditation. Then, most interestingly, she teaches about the importance of the central channel and the back body's role. She notes that many empaths' backs are closed off and the empath thus can't be open to the universe's energy and information. The reader is taught to explore the birth process, about personal trauma in early life, and about healing transgenerational trauma.

De Rosa moves the reader's attention to the second chakra, where she teaches how to heal this powerful emotional center. Here she discusses the importance of balancing the masculine and feminine, as well as exploring one's beliefs about masculinity and femininity. One journal prompt includes this: "The feminine aspect of our being includes our grounding, the seat of our emotional center, patterns of codependency, the effects of the patriarchy, the wounded masculine, and the wounded feminine. How are you connecting these many dots?" (p. 123). This powerful prompt is but one of five in this area.

By chapter 13 (of a total of 16 chapters), the reader is able to work deeply with the third chakra to access the power there.

> "If the root chakra is contracted in our childhood because of fear and lack of safety, the grounding cord underdevelops or can even become detached ... this shifts the second chakra into a state of hypervigilance and creates an imbalance in our emotional center. The third chakra region also tries to compensate by grounding to jobs, material objects, people ... like being in a freefall and grasping at anything that might help slow your fall. Sending cords into other people's chakras where there is not enough life force in your own chakras ..." (p. 129)

Other people can cord the empath as well. She notes it is so important to clear these cords and imprints because it is in the third chakra where that divine hand is at one's "back, nudging us forward in life to manifest one's true self ... to take in the current of grace that is flowing down the back side of your energy body" (p. 30).

This is a well-written and well-organized book. It also provides the reader a significantly deeper and more loving burrowing into our emotional lives than many other books of this type. This is a truly fine book for each of us as individuals to work through slowly and carefully, and an important one for practitioners. As noted earlier, it is a powerful book. In it are some astonishing and singularly eye-popping ideas—everyone deserves to discover that current of grace flowing down their backs.

Carol Atkinson, PhD, is a professor of digital media specializing in free speech, gender in the media, and personal interests in the myriad levels of consciousness. Email: atkinson@ucmo.edu

Clearing the Path: The Yoga Way to a Clear and Pleasant Mind—Patanjali, Neuroscience, and Emotion

Stephen Parker, PsyD

AHYMSA Publishers, 2017
Softcover, 368 pages
$24.95
ISBN: 978-1940629025

Reviewed by Charles B. Crenshaw Jr.

This book is an extraordinary find based on the fact that very few people have the background of the author. Stephen Parker is a man who has, like several others—notably Daniel Goleman and John Kabat-Zinn—taken their practice and understanding of meditation and done something extraordinary with it. His work is another body of useful information that has the potential to help people change their lives for the better.

What Dr. Parker has done over 12 chapters and appendices is take the ancient understanding of the mind, or mind-field, as Parker uses the ancient term, and show the relationship between that and modern neuroscience and the field of psychotherapeutic change work. It cannot be emphasized enough how rare it is to find a practitioner deeply learned in the field of psychology/psychotherapy, a serious practitioner of meditation, and someone steeped in the science of yoga. This masterful work displays Dr. Parker's wherewithal in these areas to make connections for the reader.

The specific focus of Dr. Parker's efforts, as the subtitle indicates, is providing an understanding for a way to attain "a clear and pleasant mind," something we need more of in these times. He uses a western scientific definition of mind extracted from the works of Daniel Siegel, MD, and explains how the mind is a pliable field susceptible to change, relating this to the brain's neuroplasticity. Dr. Parker is clear, however, that the modern understanding of mind is a bit different from the direct experiential understanding that meditation masters have. He also notes the subjective nature of this exercise in understanding.

Dr. Parker brings case situations to his topics to illustrate certain points and he is not shy about baring personal experience in his own efforts to achieve a clear and pleasant mind. In one chapter, he helps the reader understand when and why a meditation practitioner might need or require a mental health professional in life, and how one might go about selecting this professional. He also is holistic in his approach by addressing, if only briefly, modalities such as homeopathy and ayurveda. All this is by way of providing resources for the reader to, again, move toward a clear and pleasant mind.

Appendix A provides exercises for developing subtle awareness of the body, from relaxation exercises to breathing practices, from journaling on self-awareness about pain in the body to "sociograms" to help one work on relationships.

Dr. Parker helps us understand that developing a clear and pleasant mind is a prerequisite for progressing to true meditation and for simply having a happier life.

Although addressed to students of meditation, both beginning and advanced, this book is a fountain of knowledge for all. It introduces little-known facts about meditation as taught in the classic meditation text of Patanjali, *The Yoga Sutras.* Parker's work clarifies that yoga (the term synonymous with meditation, per Patanjali) transcends the popular exercise paradigms and fashion showcased in the media, and reaches back to humanity's quest for the nature of reality—whenever in the hoary annals of time that quest began.

Charles Crenshaw Jr., MS, is a lifelong meditator and meditation teacher, Interfaith minister, consulting hypnotist (trainer of hypnotists), neuro-linguistic programming trainer, and EFT practitioner. He is also author of Pathless Path: God, Grace, Guru, *coauthor of* EFT for Meditation, *and contributing author to* The Clinical EFT Handbook. *Email: charles@toolsforjoyfulliving.com*

Healing with Nature: Mindfulness and Somatic Practices to Heal from Trauma

Rochelle Calvert, PhD

New World Library, 2021
Softcover, 288 pages
$18.95
ISBN: 978-1608687367

Reviewed by Stephen Parker

For some years now I have led an annual silent retreat in the Lithuanian countryside with yoga meditation students there. As I have gotten to know my Lithuanian friends, one of the things I admire about them is that when they have a problem, their first impulse is to go for a walk in the woods. And Lithuania is a country of woods and lakes, not unlike my home in Minnesota. This natural draw to the company of trees may be attributable in part to the fact that when the country became the last "Christianized" country in Europe, unlike other places there was never a fight between the church and the old nature-inspired pagan religion, similar to those in the rest of Northern Europe. The Lithuanians have always felt this closeness to the healing power of the natural world, and the false dichotomy between the "civilized" and the "natural" world is less substantial.

Calvert's book seeks to help the reader reestablish this kind of familiarity with nature in the interest of healing trauma. It uses mindfulness practices, based on mindful observation, relaxation, and *metta* (Sanskrit, *maitri*) meditative affirmations to open awareness gradually and make it more and more a part of the healing process. This is combined with practices of somatic experiencing a la Peter Levine (*In an Unspoken Voice: How the Body Releases Trauma and Restores Goodness*, North Atlantic Books, 2010).

The first chapter on breath awareness contains several exercises in fundamental breath awareness. I use the term "fundamental" advisedly because it might seem as though there is such a thing as "advanced" or "expert" breath awareness. One of the secrets of mindfulness practice is that the most advanced results come from a continual refinement of the fundamentals rather than from so-called advanced technique.

Calvert appropriately cautions people who suffer panic attacks to approach these practices gently at first, as in some people these practices can trigger panic reactions. This caution aside, it seemed in the remainder of the book that she doesn't say much to help people whose traumatic experiences leave them triggered by relaxation and any sense of openness, vulnerability, or "letting go." She might consider doing more about this in successive editions. In this regard, a helpful addition to the exercises might be the yogic posture known as the crocodile, or *makarasana*, where one lies on one's stomach with legs apart and forehead resting on the forearms or wrists or one fist on top of the other (to regulate the distance between the face and the ground). In this posture, with the elbows above the levels of the shoulders, the intercostal muscles are locked in place so that anxiety-provoking chest breathing cannot happen and one gets a clear experience of feeling the movement of the diaphragm. I have used this with clients to alleviate panic attacks.

Healing with Nature is a fine, gentle, and general guide to using a natural, ecological context as a tool in healing trauma. Even as a potential patient, I would appreciate a little more explanation about the neuroscience behind why certain practices are important. I have found over many years of working with trauma survivors that these explanations provide us with a brain map for what the body is doing and this can often assist in efforts to entrain the central nervous system in positive ways. For example, Calvert mentions how the nervous system is biased towards responding to threat. These threat avoidance sequences are wired via neural networks very swiftly. To wire in a positive and relaxing experience of the sort that she is evoking requires "wallowing" in the good feelings for an extended period, at least 90 seconds or, even better, several minutes. This is, again, a suggestion for successive editions.

Calvert describes a particular canyon in California where she pursued many of these practices. The practices would be more challenging for those of us who live in winter climates, although I have to testify that it *can* be done. Like my Lithuanian friends, I find a particular grace in the woods in deep winter, a sense of purity and deep, swaddling, contemplative silence.

All of the contemplative disciplines contribute strongly to healing from trauma. The mindfulness basis of this book is sound, gentle, and useful. I would encourage the author to take us further into the details of the neuroscience behind the effectiveness of the practices as a way to deepen their positive contribution to our clients' healing.

Stephen Parker, PsyD, LP, C-IAYT, is a licensed psychologist and adjunct assistant school professor of Counseling and Psychological Services at Saint Mary's University of Minnesota, and was grandparented in 2017 as a Certified Yoga Therapist by the International Association of Yoga Therapy. A senior teacher in the Himalayan Yoga Tradition, he is the author of Clearing the Path: The Yoga Way to a Clear and Pleasant Mind. *Email: parkpsych@yahoo.com*

The energy of energy psychology

Feinstein, D. (2022). The energy of energy psychology. *OBM Integrative and Complementary Medicine, 7*(2), 28. doi:10.21926/obm.icm.2202015

Abstract

The vague or controversial use of the term energy in the clinical subdiscipline known as "energy psychology" has been an obstacle to the field's acceptance. This paper discusses five forms of energy and explores the role of each in energy psychology treatments. While patterns in (a) electrical signaling, (b) brain waves, and (c) electromagnetic fields are presumably shifted in any form of effective psychotherapy, a strength of energy psychology interventions is shown to be in their ability to initiate such effects in a deliberate and targeted manner. This paper examines the roles of these three well-established energy forms in explaining the rapid and durable outcomes seen with a wide range of conditions following energy psychology treatments. A fourth form of energy, "subtle energy," is by definition too subtle for detection by conventional scientific instruments. These energies have, however, been recognized in at least 97 healing traditions around the world and are considered to be the infrastructure of the body's physiological processes. Skepticism about subtle energies has, nonetheless, caused many critics to reject an energy psychology approach entirely, ignoring the substantial evidence base supporting it. Even more speculative are quantum influences that occur within energy psychology treatments, yet preliminary evidence for these dynamics, such as healing from a distance, has been accumulating. Although the more speculative mechanisms associated with energy psychology remain controversial, the measurable electromagnetic effects that have been shown to affect psychological states strongly support the use of the term "energy psychology."

ADDICTION/HABITS

Effect of Emotional Freedom Techniques on psychological symptoms and cravings among patients with substance related disorders

Balha, S. M., Abo-Baker, O., & Mahmoud, S. (2020). Effect of Emotional Freedom Techniques on psychological symptoms and cravings among patients with substance related disorders. *International Journal of Novel Research in Healthcare and Nursing, 7*(2), 30–45.

Abstract

Background: Numerous researchers have found a recurrent co-occurrence of cravings and psychological distress among addiction patients. Thus, this necessitates applying an evidence-based practice such as Emotional Freedom Techniques (EFT), which is characterized by simplicity and can be used as a self-help tool for managing cravings and psychological symptoms such as anxiety and depression.

Aim: This study aimed to assess the effect of EFT on psychological symptoms and cravings among patients with substance related disorders.

Design: Quasi experimental research design was used.

Setting: The present study was conducted at Elmaamoura Hospital for Psychiatric Medicine in Alexandria, Egypt.

Subjects: The subjects of the study comprised 90 patients.

Tools: Three tools were used: Tool I, Interview questionnaire sheet (sociodemographic and clinical data); Tool II, for substance related disorders and alcohol cravings, Penn Alcohol Craving Scale (PACS); and Tool III, Symptom Checklist 90 scale (SCL-90 R).

Results: Applying the psycho-educational program of EFT significantly reduced levels of craving. Statistically significant decreases were observed in the three global indices (GSI, PSDI, PST) and all nine dimensions of the SCL-90 subscales after the sessions, indicating a reduction in psychological distress ($p < .005$).

Conclusion: Applying the psycho-educational program of EFT significantly reduces levels of craving, with significant improvements in psychological symptoms among substance related disorders patients.

Recommendations: These results demonstrate that EFT could be an efficient adjunct tool for addiction treatment by reducing the high levels of craving and decreasing severity of the general psychological symptom distress among addiction patients.

Skinny Genes' six-week, online, clinical Emotional Freedom Techniques program: Durable weight loss and improved psychological symptoms

Church, D., Stapleton, P., & Raynor, D. (2022). Skinny Genes' six-week, online, clinical Emotional Freedom Techniques program: Durable weight loss and improved psychological symptoms. *Advances, 36*(1), 13–21.

Abstract

Context: With obesity a mounting global issue, efficacious treatments can make a contribution to both personal and public health. Prior clinical trials have demonstrated that an evidence-based method, Clinical Emotional Freedom Techniques (EFT), can produce a durable weight reduction.

Objective: The study evaluated whether Skinny Genes, a six-week online program applying EFT to emotional eating, was associated with behavioral change and reductions in weight.

Design: A pre-post outcome study design evaluated the results of a convenience sample of participants enrolled in an online weight loss course.

Participants: Participant were recruited through EFT websites. Pre, post, and follow-up measures were available for 72 participants and all analysis was performed on this sample.

Intervention: Participants used EFT to address cognitions, behaviors, and adverse experiences that could contribute to binge eating, intermittent dieting, and resistance to exercise.

Outcome Measures: Behaviors to restrain eating were measured using the Revised Restraint Scale (RRS), the association of food with reward using the Power of Food Scale (PFS), and anxiety and depression using the Hospital Anxiety and Depression Scale (HADS). Weight was measured pre and postintervention and at six-month follow-up.

Results: Postintervention, a 36.8% reduction in anxiety ($p < .001$) and a 48.5% reduction in depression ($p < .001$) were found. The perceived power of food decreased significantly as did restraint behaviors. Participants lost an average of 12.9 pounds during the six weeks of the program ($p < .001$), and at follow-up, a further 2.6 pounds. All psychological gains were maintained ($p < .001$).

Conclusions: The findings are consistent with those of other clinical trials studying the benefits of EFT for weight loss, demonstrating simultaneous reductions in both weight and psychological distress. The continued weight reduction found on follow-up was consistent with other EFT studies but counter to the pattern of weight regain noted in the literature. Addressing emotional issues using an online delivery format was associated with durable weight-loss maintenance as well as improved mental health. App-based and virtual programs such as Skinny Genes have the potential to bring effective therapies to underserved populations.

Addiction treatment and telehealth: Review of efficacy and provider insights during the COVID-19 pandemic

Mark, T. L., Treiman, K., Padwa, H., Henretty, K., Tzeng, J., & Gilbert, M. (2021). Addiction treatment and telehealth: Review of efficacy and provider insights during the COVID-19 pandemic. *Psychiatric Services, 2021.* doi:10.1176/appi.ps.202100088

Abstract

Objective: Addiction treatment via telehealth expanded to unprecedented levels during the COVID-19 pandemic. This study aimed to clarify whether the research evidence on the efficacy of telehealth-delivered substance use disorder treatment and the experience of providers using telehealth during the pandemic support continued use of telehealth after the pandemic and, if so, under what circumstances.

Methods: Data sources included a literature review on the efficacy of telehealth for substance use disorder treatment, responses to a 2020 online survey from 100 California addiction treatment providers, and interviews with 30 California treatment providers and other stakeholders.

Results: Eight published studies were identified that compared addiction treatment via telehealth with in-person treatment. Seven found telehealth treatment as effective but not more effective than in-person treatment in terms of retention, therapeutic alliance, and substance use. One Canadian study found that telehealth facilitated methadone prescribing and improved retention. In the survey results reported here, California addiction treatment providers said that more than 50% of their patients were being treated via telehealth for intensive outpatient treatment, individual counseling, group counseling, and intake assessment. They were most confident that individual counseling via telehealth was as effective as in-person individual counseling and less sure about the relative effectiveness of telehealth-delivered medication management, group counseling, and intake assessments.

Conclusions: Telehealth may help engage patients in addiction treatment by improving access and convenience. Additional research is needed to confirm that benefit and to determine how best to tailor telehealth to each patient's circumstances and with what mix of in-person and telehealth services.

Dietary ethanol ingestion by free-ranging spider monkeys (*Ateles geoffroyi*)

Campbell, C. J., Maro, A., Weaver, V., & Dudley, R. (2022). Dietary ethanol ingestion by free-ranging spider monkeys (*Ateles geoffroyi*). *Royal Society Open Science, 9*(3), 211729. doi:10.1098/rsos.211729

Abstract

Ethanol within ripe and over-ripe fruit is produced naturally through the metabolic activity of fermentative yeasts. As a consequence, frugivorous animals may chronically consume ethanol as part of their routine diet, although direct measurements of such exposure are lacking. Here, we present data on ethanol concentrations within fruits of *Spondias mombin* (Anacardiaceae) that are eaten by black-handed spider monkeys (*Ateles geoffroyi*) on Barro Colorado Island, Panama. Of collected fruits that were partially consumed and then dropped by foraging monkeys, pulp-ethanol content was typically in the range of 1%–2%; the percentage of pulp for consumed fruits was not significantly correlated with the ethanol concentration of the pulp remaining within each fruit. Urine samples from foraging spider monkeys were also evaluated for the ethanol metabolites ethyl glucuronide and ethyl sulfate; five of six samples tested positive for both compounds. In aggregate, these data indicate natural exposure to fruit-associated ethanol in a wild primate species.

Microglial activation states drive glucose uptake and FDG-PET alterations in neurodegenerative diseases

Xiang, X., Wind, K., Wiedemann, T., Blume, T., Shi, Y., Briel, N., . . . Brendel, M. (2021). Microglial activation states drive glucose uptake and FDG-PET alterations in neurodegenerative diseases. *Science Translational Medicine, 13*(615), eabe5640. doi:10.1126/scitranslmed.abe5640

Abstract

2-Deoxy-2-[^{18}F]fluoro-D-glucose positron emission tomography (FDG-PET) is widely used to study cerebral glucose metabolism. Here, we investigated whether the FDG-PET signal is directly influenced by microglial glucose uptake in mouse models and patients with neurodegenerative diseases. Using a recently developed approach for cell sorting after FDG injection, we found that, at cellular resolution, microglia displayed higher glucose uptake than neurons and astrocytes. Alterations in microglial glucose uptake were responsible for both the FDG-PET signal decrease in *Trem2*-deficient mice and the FDG-PET signal increase in mouse models for amyloidosis. Thus, opposite microglial activation states determine the differential FDG uptake. Consistently, 12 patients with Alzheimer's disease and 21 patients with four-repeat tauopathies also exhibited a positive association between glucose uptake and microglial activity as determined by ^{18}F-GE-180 18-kDa translocator protein PET (TSPO-PET) in preserved brain regions, indicating that the cerebral glucose uptake in humans is also strongly influenced by microglial activity. Our findings suggest that microglia activation states are responsible for FDG-PET signal alterations in patients with neurodegenerative diseases and mouse models for amyloidosis. Microglial activation states should therefore be considered when performing FDG-PET.

A salient sugar tax decreases sugary-drink buying

Donnelly, G. E., Guge, P. M., Howell, R. T., & John, L. K. (2021). A salient sugar tax decreases sugary-drink buying. *Psychological Science, 32*(11), 1830–1841. doi:10.1177/09567976211017022

Abstract

Many governments have introduced sugary-drink excise taxes to reduce purchasing and consumption of such drinks; however, they do not typically stipulate how such taxes should be communicated at the point of purchase. Historical, field, and experimental data consisting of more than 225,000 purchase decisions indicated that introducing a $0.01-per-ounce sugar-sweetened beverage (SSB) tax—without making it salient on price tags—had no significant effect on purchasing (−1.26%, $p = .28$). However, when the phrase "includes sugary drink tax" was added to tax-inclusive price tags, SSB purchasing was lower than (a) in the pretax period (−9.78%, $p < .001$), (b) in a posttax period when drinks did not bear price tags (−5.04%, $p < .001$), and (c) in a posttax period when drinks bore tax-inclusive price tags that did not mention the tax (−3.83%, $p = .002$). Making the tax's beneficiary (student programs) salient on price tags had no added effect. Two follow-up studies suggested that tax salience was effective partly because consumers overestimated the tax amount, leading to reduced purchase intentions.

Longitudinal analysis of neighborhood food environment and diabetes risk in the Veterans Administration Diabetes Risk cohort

Kanchi, R., Lopez, P., Rummo, P. E., Lee, D. C., Adhikari, S., Schwartz, M. D., . . . Thorpe, L. E. (2021). Longitudinal analysis of neighborhood food environment and diabetes risk in the Veterans Administration Diabetes Risk cohort. *JAMA Network Open, 4*(10), e2130789–e2130789. doi:10.1001/jamanetworkopen.2021.30789

Abstract

Importance: Diabetes causes substantial morbidity and mortality among adults in the US, yet its incidence varies across the country, suggesting that neighborhood factors are associated with geographical disparities in diabetes.

Objective: To examine the association between neighborhood food environment and risk of incident type 2 diabetes across different community types (high-density urban, low-density urban, suburban, and rural).

Design, setting, and participants: This is a national cohort study of 4,100,650 US veterans without type 2 diabetes. Participants entered the cohort between 2008 and 2016 and were followed up through 2018. The median (IQR) duration of follow-up was 5.5 (2.6–9.8) person-years. Data were obtained from Veterans Affairs electronic health records. Incident type 2 diabetes was defined as two encounters with type 2 diabetes International Classification of Diseases, Ninth Revision or Tenth Revision codes, a prescription for diabetes medication other than metformin or acarbose alone, or one encounter with type 2 diabetes International Classification of Diseases Ninth Revision or Tenth Revision codes and two instances of elevated hemoglobin A1c (≥6.5%). Data analysis was performed from October 2020 to March 2021.

Exposures: Five-year mean counts of fast-food restaurants and supermarkets relative to other food outlets at baseline were used to generate neighborhood food environment measures. The association between food environment and time to incident diabetes was examined using piecewise exponential models with two-year interval of person-time and county-level random effects stratifying by community types.

Results: The mean (SD) age of cohort participants was 59.4 (17.2) years. Most of the participants were non-Hispanic White (2,783,756 participants [76.3%]) and male (3,779,555 participants [92.2%]). The relative density of fast-food restaurants was positively associated with a modestly increased risk of type 2 diabetes in all community types. The adjusted hazard ratio (aHR) was 1.01 (95% CI, 1.00–1.02) in high-density urban communities, 1.01 (95% CI, 1.01–1.01) in low-density urban communities, 1.02 (95% CI, 1.01–1.03) in suburban communities, and 1.01 (95% CI, 1.01–1.02) in rural communities. The relative density of supermarkets was associated with lower type 2 diabetes risk only in suburban (aHR, 0.97; 95% CI, 0.96–0.99) and rural (aHR, 0.99; 95% CI, 0.98–0.99) communities.

Conclusions and relevance: These findings suggest that neighborhood food environment measures are associated with type 2 diabetes among US veterans in multiple community types and that food environments are potential avenues for action to address the burden of diabetes. Tailored interventions targeting the availability of supermarkets may be associated with reduced diabetes risk, particularly in suburban and rural communities, whereas restrictions on fast-food restaurants may help in all community types.

ANXIETY/DEPRESSION

Effect of EFT tapping on anxiety and quality of life

Warrier, A. (2018). Effect of EFT tapping on anxiety and quality of life. *Phonix International Journal for Psychology and Social Sciences (PIJPS), 2*(2), 53–73.

Abstract

Emotional Freedom Technique (EFT) as a new therapeutic technique in energy psychology has positive effects on psychological and physiological symptoms, and quality of life. It has deep roots in modern psychology as well as the ancient science of acupuncture. It is also called tapping because EFT involves tapping with your fingertips on acupoints on your body. Studies were conducted to understand the effect of EFT Tapping on anxiety and quality of life in adults. Ethical approval was secured. Clients over the age of 20 years and staying in the Delhi NCR area were invited to participate in a two-week intervention program. At the start and end of their intervention, participants were asked to complete STAT and WHOQOL-BREF questionnaires. Sixty-five participants gave consent, 61 completed questionnaires, and 46 fulfilled the inclusion criteria. The range in age was 20–75 years. The researcher conducted three tapping sessions in a time span of two weeks. The main presenting conditions were anxiety. STAT and WHOQOL-BREF scores showed both emotionally and statistically significant improvements after the intervention. Statistically there was significant improvement for anxiety and quality of life (all $p < .001$). Mean anxiety scores improved from 8.3250 (high) at start to 6.9750 (average). Mean quality of life scores improved from 65.5313 at start to 67.1125 (higher mean shows better quality of life) at end (SD = 6.81, $p < .001$). Improvements were seen in all participants. Despite the limited sample size and other limitations, significant improvements were shown. The results support the potential of EFT as a cost-effective intervention to reduce anxiety and thereby help improve quality of life. However, there were few data available comparing EFT to standard-of-care treatments such as cognitive behavioral therapy, and further research is needed to establish the relative efficacy of EFT to established protocols.

Effects on anxiety and vital signs of the Emotional Freedom Technique and music before surgery for lumbar disc hernia

Cici, R., & Özkan, M. (2021). Effects on anxiety and vital signs of the Emotional Freedom Technique and music before surgery for lumbar disc hernia. *Alternative Therapies in Health and Medicine, 27*(12).

Context: Patients hospitalized for surgical treatment for lumbar disc herniation (LDH) are adversely affected psychologically, with fury, anger, helplessness, anxiety, and depression being observed in patients. Anxiety in particular is a common problem, with an incidence of around 90%.

Objective: This study intended to determine the effects on patients' anxiety and vital signs of the Emotional Freedom Technique (EFT) and music before LDH surgery.

Design: The research team designed a quasi-experimental study.

Setting: The research was carried out in the neurosurgery clinic of a university hospital in Turkey.

Participants: Participants were 162 adult patients at the clinic who had LDH surgery between February 2018 and September 2019.

Intervention: Using the nonprobability sampling method, participants were allocated to one of three groups: (1) 54 to the music group, an intervention group; (2) 54 patients to the EFT group, an intervention group; and (3) 54 to the control group.

Outcome Measures: The Patient Information Form, Life Findings Form, Subjective Units of Distress (SUD) scale, and State-Trait Anxiety Inventory–State Anxiety (STAI-S) were used to collect data. In the data analysis, the numbers, percentages, means, standard deviations, and chi-square values were found, and the *t*-test and an analysis of variance (ANOVA) were used in the dependent and independent groups, respectively. The Tukey test was used for further analysis.

Results: EFT and music were determined to significantly reduce participants' state anxiety and subjective discomfort ($p < .001$). EFT significantly reduced the pulse and respiratory rates and the systolic blood pressure, and music significantly lowered the diastolic and systolic blood pressures ($p < .05$). Further analyses showed that EFT was more effective on state anxiety and reducing the respiratory rate than music.

Conclusions: Both music and EFT before LDH surgery reduced anxiety and regulated vital signs, and EFT was found to be more effective than music in regulating anxiety and respiratory rate.

EFT as a tool to resolve anxiety: A case study approach

Pandey, N. (2020). EFT as a tool to resolve anxiety: A case study approach. *International Journal of Psycho-Social Research (IJPSR), 9*(1).

Abstract

Background: The present work examines the extent to which Emotional Freedom Technique (EFT) is effective as a tool in resolving anxiety. In recent years, various mental health professionals have been focusing on the use of alternative therapies like Thought Field Therapy (TFT), hypnotherapy, past life regression therapy, and Reiki, but there is a paucity of empirical research on the underlying factors for managing emotional challenges and turmoil.

Objective: One of the latest techniques, EFT, was established by Gary Craig. Case study method was used for the present case of one individual who had a very high level of anxiety.

Measures: To measure the level of anxiety, the Subjective Units of Discomfort (SUD) scale, as an introspective technique for experienced emotional and psychosomatic discomfort, was used as a pre and post measure.

Findings: Major findings were at two levels: (a) intensive effect of one traumatic event on the adult life (in this case, anger leading to performance anxiety and fear of authority), and (b) how EFT helps a person to understand and handle emotions in a positive manner. The implication of the study is that the person who practices EFT regularly would be in a better position to understand and handle disturbing emotions. It is a cost-effective, easy-to-learn, simple-to-use tapping technique that can be used anywhere, anytime, and any number of times in a day. It can be used for all emotions and body pains.

Jasubhai, S. (2021). Efficacy of Emotional Freedom Technique and cognitive behavioural therapy on stress, anxiety, depression, short-term memory, psychophysiological coherence and heart rate in Indian adults

Jasubhai, S. (2021). Efficacy of Emotional Freedom Technique and cognitive behavioural therapy on stress, anxiety, depression, short-term memory, psychophysiological coherence and heart rate in Indian adults. *Clinical Psychology and Mental Health Care, 2*(4). doi:03.2021/1.10025

Abstract

World Health Organization reported depression as the fourth leading cause of mental illness worldwide and one of the leading causes of disabilities among adults. Living with depression may cause sleep deprivation, anxiety, stress, and short-term memory loss. This is because the individual's mind may be occupied with negative thoughts. Depression affects a person's feelings, thinking, daily functioning, processing speed, memory, and executive functions. National Mental Health Survey of India in 2015–2016 reports that one in 20 Indians suffers from depression. Earlier research indicated that cognitive behavioral Therapy (CBT) represents a superior approach in treating mild to severe depression symptoms, and Emotional Freedom Technique (EFT) received increased attention. The present study is in line with a study conducted in Australia in 2016 by Hannah Chatwin et al. The objective of the current study is to evaluate the efficacy of EFT and CBT in the treatment of stress, anxiety and depression, short-term memory loss, psychophysiological coherence, and heart rate in Indian young adults. Subjects (n = 14), selected at random, from Ahmedabad (a metro city) in India, were screened for stress, anxiety, and depression using the Depression, Anxiety and Stress scale (DASS-21) and Beck Depression Inventory (BDI-2). They were also screened for short-term memory (STM) using the Digit Span test, which allowed assessments of each participant's initial complaints of forgetfulness, difficulty in concentrating, and confusion. Their psychophysiological coherence score and heart rate were recorded pre and postinterventions using the emWave system. These subjects were randomly assigned to a program of eight once-a-week CBT or EFT treatments. All participants were screened after three sessions, five sessions, eight sessions, and six months' follow-up using DASS-21, BDI-2, and Digit Span Test. They were also screened after one month for stress, anxiety, and depression using DASS-21 and BDI-2. Findings of the study depicted that both intervention approaches produced significant reductions in stress, anxiety, and depressive symptoms and concurrent improvement in short-term memory (STM), psychophysiological coherence, and heart rate. The EFT treatment produced marked improvement in depression after three sessions. After eight weeks of intervention, the CBT group reported significant improvement in depression and short-term memory, while EFT intervention therapy showed significant improvement in depression state after one month and at six months' follow-up. Examination of individual cases showed clinically significant improvement in stress, anxiety, depression symptoms, short-term memory, and psychophysiological coherence across both interventions. The results are consistent with the previous studies by Hannah Chatwin et al. (2016). Present findings suggest that EFT would be an effective intervention therapy in managing stress, anxiety, depression, and STM and worthy of further investigation.

Effects of Emotion Freedom Techniques on academic stress in Korean medical students: A single-group pre-post study

Lee, S., Han, S. Y., Lee, S. J., Chae, H., & Lim, J. (2022). Effects of Emotion Freedom Techniques on academic stress in Korean medical students: A single-group pre-post study. *Journal of Oriental Neuropsychiatry, 33*(1), 33–48. doi:10.7231/jon.2022.33.1.033

Abstract

Objectives: Academic stress poses a significant risk for the mental health of medical students, and a feasible group intervention program for managing academic stress is required. The purpose of this study was to examine the clinical effectiveness of Emotional Freedom Techniques (EFT) on the mental health of Korean medical students.

Methods: The class of first-year medical school students ($n = 36$) participated in an after-school EFT group intervention program comprising six sessions (15 minutes/session, three weeks) to analyze its clinical effectiveness as a single-group test-retest clinical study. The changes in the Perceived Stress Scale (PSS), Test Anxiety Inventory (TAI), Positive and Negative Affect Schedule (PANAS), and State-Trait Anxiety Inventory (STAI) scores were examined using a paired *t*-test and Cohen's *d* at post-EFT and two-week follow-up.

Results: There were significant curtailments at post-EFT and follow-up measures in TAI-Total ($t = 2.704$ and $t = 3.289$), TAI-Worry ($t = 2.297$ and $t = 2.454$), TAI-Emotionality ($t = 2.763$ and $t = 3.654$), PSS-Negative Perspective ($t = 2.659$ and $t = 3.877$), and PANAS-Negative Affect ($t = 2.885$ and $t = 3.259$) subscales, however, not in PSS-Positive Perspective ($t = -1.279$ and $t = -1.101$) and PANAS-Positive Affect ($t = .194$ and $t = -.122$) subscales. The trait anxiety ($t = 2.227$) was significantly mitigated in the post-EFT measure and the state anxiety ($t = 2.30$) in the follow-up measure.

Conclusions: The EFT group intervention alleviated test stress, negative affect, and anxiety in the Korean medical students. This study contributes to an understanding of academic stress and EFT intervention in the competitive environment of medical education.

Anxiety and depression among parents of children with intellectual disability in Pakistan

Azeem, M. W., Dogar, I. A., Shah, S., Cheema, M. A., Asmat, A., Akbar, M., ... Haider, I. I. (2013). Anxiety and depression among parents of children with intellectual disability in Pakistan. *Journal of the Canadian Academy of Child and Adolescent Psychiatry, 22*(4), 290–295.

Abstract

Background: Studies have shown an association between parental distress and caretaking of children with developmental cognitive delays. There is little data in developing countries, such as Pakistan, concerning the impact of raising children with intellectual disability upon the quality of parent functioning and risk for psychopathology.

Objective: To assess the level of psychopathology, i.e., anxiety, depression, and both anxiety and depression together among parents of children with intellectual disability (ID).

Methods: This was a cross-sectional study conducted at a tertiary care hospital in Pakistan. The study was approved by the Institutional Research Committee. Participants were 198 parents (99 fathers/99 mothers) of 100 children with the diagnosis of ID. Informed consents were obtained. The parents were assessed for anxiety and depression using DSM IV criteria.

Results: A significantly high proportion of mothers (89%) had anxiety, depression, or both anxiety and depression together as compared to fathers (77%) ($p < .05$). Among mothers, 35% met criteria for anxiety, 40% for depression, and 13% for both anxiety and depression. Among fathers, 42% had anxiety, 31% depression, and 3% both anxiety and depression. There was a significant association between gender of parent and individual psychiatric diagnosis of anxiety, depression, and anxiety and depression together ($p < .05$). A significant association was also found between mother's anxiety, depression, or both and degree of ID of their children ($p < .05$).

Conclusions: (1) A significantly high proportion of parents of children with ID has a psychiatric diagnosis of anxiety, depression, or both; (2) the psychiatric diagnosis of anxiety, depression, and anxiety and depression together is associated with gender of parent; and (3) the diagnosis of anxiety, depression, or both in mothers was associated with severity of ID in their children.

The effects of a Thought Field Therapy stress reduction protocol on the stress and empathy levels of parents of children with Autism Spectrum Disorder

Keppel, H. (2021). *The effects of a Thought Field Therapy stress reduction protocol on the stress and empathy levels of parents of children with Autism Spectrum Disorder.* (Doctoral dissertation, Fielding Graduate University). Retrieved from Proquest.

Abstract
The effects of a stress reduction Thought Field Therapy (TFT) protocol vs. a control-stimulation protocol on general stress, parenting stress, and empathy (perspective taking) were explored in this mixed-model, randomized control study. Parents of children with autism, from Israel and the USA, showed reduced general stress and an increase in perspective taking following the intervention, as measured by self-reports. Parenting stress partially mediated the effect of TFT on perspective taking. There were no additional changes during the follow-up period. Participants with personality characteristics of the broad autism phenotype (BAP) presented at baseline higher general and parenting-related stress scores, and lower perspective taking scores, regardless of their intervention group. The finding suggests that perspective taking is part of the broad autism phenotype. TFT was effective, regardless of participants' BAP status.

Effectiveness of EFT on suicidal ideation among young adults

Patel, V., & Pandey, N. (2021). Effectiveness of EFT on suicidal ideation among young adults. *International Journal of Indian Psychology, 9*(3). doi:10.25215/0903.192

Abstract
The present study examines the effectiveness of Emotional Freedom Technique (EFT) as an intervention for suicidal ideation among young adults. Suicide has been documented in various literature wherein its definition has constantly changed, as has the definition of suicidal ideation. As a result, there is no universally accepted consistent definition for either. An enormous part of our society, including the young adults, commits suicide every year. The current situation calls for an easily assessable and effective intervention that can be implemented to deal with suicidal ideation as suicide prevention. Respondents between the age of 18 and 40 years were assessed for the presence of suicidal ideation using Columbia-Suicide Severity Rating Scale at the beginning and end of intervention. Eight participants out of 20 respondents were provided with intervention. Participants were given an initial EFT session to gain better insight into their distress issues that lead to suicidal ideation and to provide them with understanding of how EFT is conducted. Participants were then instructed to practice EFT on themselves on a daily basis for the next 21 days. In postintervention assessment, EFT not only proved to be effective in reducing suicidal ideation, but it also provided participants with necessary insight, created and enhanced self-love, and made them self-aware and efficient in handling their emotions. EFT is a cost-effective, easy-to-use technique that can be employed for all emotions and physical pain anytime, anywhere, and any number of times.

Frequent interpersonal stress and inflammatory reactivity predict depressive-symptom increases: Two tests of the social-signal-transduction theory of depression

Madison, A. A., Andridge, R., Shrout, M. R., Renna, M. E., Bennett, J. M., Jaremka, L. M., . . . Kiecolt-Glaser, J. K. (2021). Frequent interpersonal stress and inflammatory reactivity predict depressive-symptom increases: Two tests of the social-signal-transduction theory of depression. *Psychological Science, 33*(1), 152–164. doi:10.1177/09567976211031225

Abstract

The social-signal-transduction theory of depression asserts that people who experience ongoing interpersonal stressors and mount a greater inflammatory response to social stress are at higher risk for depression. The current study tested this theory in two adult samples. In Study 1, physically healthy adults ($N = 76$) who reported more frequent interpersonal tension had heightened depressive symptoms at Visit 2, but only if they had greater inflammatory reactivity to a marital conflict at Visit 1. Similarly, in Study 2, depressive symptoms increased among lonelier and less socially supported breast-cancer survivors ($N = 79$). This effect was most pronounced among participants with higher inflammatory reactivity to a social-evaluative stressor at Visit 1. In both studies, noninterpersonal stress did not interact with inflammatory reactivity to predict later depressive symptoms.

Increased global integration in the brain after psilocybin therapy for depression

Daws, R. E., Timmermann, C., Giribaldi, B., Sexton, J. D., Wall, M. B., Erritzoe, D., . . . Carhart-Harris, R. (2022). Increased global integration in the brain after psilocybin therapy for depression. *Nature Medicine, 28,* 844–851. doi:10.1038/s41591-022-01744-z

Abstract

Psilocybin therapy shows antidepressant potential, but its therapeutic actions are not well understood. We assessed the subacute impact of psilocybin on brain function in two clinical trials of depression. The first was an open-label trial of orally administered psilocybin (10 mg and 25 mg, 7 days apart) in patients with treatment-resistant depression. Functional magnetic resonance imaging (fMRI) was recorded at baseline and one day after the 25-mg dose. Beck's Depression Inventory was the primary outcome measure (MR/J00460X/1). The second trial was a double-blind phase II randomized controlled trial comparing psilocybin therapy with escitalopram. Patients with major depressive disorder received either 2 × 25 mg oral psilocybin, 3 weeks apart, plus 6 weeks of daily placebo ("psilocybin arm") or 2 × 1 mg oral psilocybin, 3 weeks apart, plus 6 weeks of daily escitalopram, 10–20 mg ("escitalopram arm"). fMRI was recorded at baseline and three weeks after the second psilocybin dose (NCT03429075). In both trials, the antidepressant response to psilocybin was rapid, sustained, and correlated with decreases in fMRI brain network modularity, implying that psilocybin's antidepressant action may depend on a global increase in brain network integration. Network cartography analyses indicated that 5-HT2A receptor-rich higher-order functional networks became more functionally interconnected and flexible after psilocybin treatment. The antidepressant response to escitalopram was milder and no changes in brain network organization were observed. Consistent efficacy-related brain changes, correlating with robust antidepressant effects across two studies, suggest an antidepressant mechanism for psilocybin therapy: global increases in brain network integration.

ATTITUDES/BELIEFS

Bigotry and the human-animal divide: (Dis)belief in human evolution and bigoted attitudes across different cultures

Syropoulos, S., Lifshin, U., Greenberg, J., Horner, D. E., & Leidner, B. (2022). Bigotry and the human-animal divide: (Dis)belief in human evolution and bigoted attitudes across different cultures. *Journal of Personality and Social Psychology.* Advance online publication. doi:10.1037/pspi0000391

Abstract

The current investigation tested if people's basic belief in the notion that human beings have developed from other animals (i.e., belief in evolution) can predict human-to-human prejudice and intergroup hostility. Using data from the American General Social Survey and Pew Research Center (Studies 1–4) and from three online samples (Studies 5, 7, 8), we tested this hypothesis across 45 countries, in diverse populations and religious settings, across time, in nationally representative data ($N = 60{,}703$), and with more comprehensive measures in online crowdsourced data ($N = 2{,}846$). Supporting the hypothesis, low belief in human evolution was associated with higher levels of prejudice, racist attitudes, and support for discriminatory behaviors against Lesbian, Gay, Bisexual, Transgender, and Queer (LGBTQ), Blacks, and immigrants in the United States (Study 1), with higher ingroup biases, prejudicial attitudes toward outgroups, and less support for conflict resolution in samples collected from 19 Eastern European countries (Study 2), 25 Muslim countries (Study 3), and Israel (Study 4). Further, among Americans, lower belief in evolution was associated with greater prejudice and militaristic attitudes toward political outgroups (Study 5). Finally, perceived similarity to animals (a construct distinct from belief in evolution, Study 6) partially mediated the link between belief in evolution and prejudice (Studies 7 and 8), even when controlling for religious beliefs, political views, and other demographic variables, and was also observed for nondominant groups (i.e., religious and racial minorities). Overall, these findings highlight the importance of belief in human evolution as a potentially key individual-difference variable predicting racism and prejudice.

Changes in Americans' prejudices during the presidency of Donald Trump

Ruisch, B. C., & Ferguson, M. J. (2022). Changes in Americans' prejudices during the presidency of Donald Trump. *Nature Human Behaviour*, 1–10. doi:10.1038/s41562-021-01287-2

Abstract

The presidency of Donald Trump represented a relatively unique event in modern American history, whereby a sitting US president made numerous controversial remarks about minoritized groups yet nonetheless maintained substantial public support. Trump's comments constituted a departure from the egalitarian norms that had long characterized American political discourse. Here, we examine the potential effects of Trump's rhetoric on Americans' attitudes, predicting that these high-profile norm violations may have reshaped the personal prejudices of the American people. In 13 studies including over 10,000 participants, we tested how Americans' prejudice changed following the political ascension of Donald Trump. We found that explicit racial and religious prejudice significantly increased amongst Trump's supporters, whereas individuals opposed to Trump exhibited decreases in prejudice. Further, changing social norms appear to explain these changes in prejudice. These results suggest that Trump's presidency coincided with a substantial change in the topography of prejudice in the United States.

Childhood cross-ethnic exposure predicts political behavior seven decades later: Evidence from linked administrative data

Brown, J. R., Enos, R. D., Feigenbaum, J., & Mazumder, S. (2021). Childhood cross-ethnic exposure predicts political behavior seven decades later: Evidence from linked administrative data. *Science Advances, 7*(24), eabe8432. doi:10.1126/sciadv.abe8432

Abstract

Does contact across social groups influence sociopolitical behavior? This question is among the most studied in the social sciences with deep implications for the harmony of diverse societies. Yet, despite a voluminous body of scholarship, evidence around this question is limited to cross-sectional surveys that only measure short-term consequences of contact or to panel surveys with small samples covering short time periods. Using advances in machine learning that enable large-scale linkages across datasets, we examine the long-term determinants of sociopolitical behavior through an unprecedented individual-level analysis linking contemporary political records to the 1940 U.S. Census. These linked data allow us to measure the exact residential context of nearly every person in the United States in 1940 and, for men, connect this with the political behavior of those still alive over 70 years later. We find that, among white Americans, early-life exposure to black neighbors predicts Democratic partisanship over 70 years later.

Little evidence for sex or ovarian hormone influences on affective variability

Weigard, A., Loviska, A. M., & Beltz, A. M. (2021). Little evidence for sex or ovarian hormone influences on affective variability. *Scientific Reports, 11*(1), 1–12. doi:10.1038/s41598-021-00143-7

Abstract

Women were historically excluded from research participation partly due to the assumption that ovarian hormone fluctuations lead to variation, especially in emotion, that could not be experimentally controlled. Although challenged in principle and practice, relevant empirical data are limited by single measurement occasions. The current paper fills this knowledge gap using data from a 75-day intensive longitudinal study. Three indices of daily affective variability—volatility, emotional inertia, and cyclicity—were evaluated using Bayesian inferential methods in 142 men, naturally cycling women, and women using three different oral contraceptive formulations (that "stabilize" hormone fluctuations). Results provided more evidence for similarities between men and women—and between naturally cycling women and oral contraceptive users—than for differences. Even if differences exist, effects are likely small. Thus, there is little indication that ovarian hormones influence affective variability in women to a greater extent than the biopsychosocial factors that influence daily emotion in men.

Reconciling well-being and resilience for sustainable development

Chaigneau, T., Coulthard, S., Daw, T. M., Szaboova, L., Camfield, L., Chapin, F. S., . . . Brown, K. (2022). Reconciling well-being and resilience for sustainable development. *Nature Sustainability, 5*(4), 287–293. doi:10.1038/s41893-021-00790-8

Abstract

Securing well-being and building resilience in response to shocks are often viewed as key goals of sustainable development. Here, we present an overview of the latest published evidence, as well as the consensus of a diverse group of scientists and practitioners drawn from a structured analytical review and deliberative workshop process. We argue that resilience and well-being are related in complex ways, but in their applications in practice they are often assumed to be synergistic. Although theoretically compatible, evidence we present here shows that they may in fact work against each other. This has important implications for policy.

'I get high with a little help from my friends'—how raves can invoke identity fusion and lasting co-operation via transformative experiences

Newson, M., Khurana, R., Cazorla, F., & van Mulukom, V. (2021). 'I get high with a little help from my friends'—how raves can invoke identity fusion and lasting co-operation via transformative experiences. *Frontiers in Psychology, 4303.* doi:10.3389/fpsyg.2021.719596

Abstract

Psychoactive drugs have been central to many human group rituals throughout modern human evolution. Despite such experiences often being inherently social, bonding and associated prosocial behaviors have rarely been empirically tested as an outcome. Here we investigate a novel measure of the mechanisms that generate altered states of consciousness during group rituals, the 4Ds: *d*ance, *d*rums, sleep *d*eprivation, and *d*rugs. We conducted a retrospective online survey examining experiences at a highly ritualized cultural phenomenon where drug use is relatively uninhibited—raves and illegal free parties. Engaging in the 4Ds at raves or free parties was associated with personal transformation for those who experienced the event as awe-inspiring, especially for people with open personalities ($n = 481$). Without awe, or a ritual context, indulging in the 4Ds was associated with a lack of personal growth, or anomie. A complex SEM revealed that personal transformation following awe-inspiring raves was associated with bonding to other ravers and prosocial behavior toward this group at a cost to self in a simple economic game. Bonding to humanity was not associated with these events. The findings suggest that employing the 4Ds in a ritualized environment—particularly dancing and drug use—can help build meaningful social bonds with associated positive behavioral outcomes.

The development of speciesism: Age-related differences in the moral view of animals

McGuire, L., Palmer, S. B., & Faber, N. S. (2022). The development of speciesism: Age-related differences in the moral view of animals. *Social Psychological and Personality Science*, 194855062210861. doi:10.1177/19485506221086182

Abstract
Humans care for the well-being of some animals (e.g., dogs) yet tacitly endorse the maltreatment of others (e.g., pigs). What treatment is deemed morally appropriate for an animal can depend on whether the animal is characterized as "food." When such categorization of animals emerges and when a moral hierarchy of beings depending on their species membership (speciesism) develops is poorly understood. We investigate this development across samples of children (9–11 years old), young adults (18–21 years old), and adults (29–59 years old; total $N = 479$). Compared with young adults and adults, children (a) show less speciesism, (b) are less likely to categorize farm animals as food than pets, (c) think farm animals ought to be treated better, and (d) deem eating meat and animal products to be less morally acceptable. These findings imply that there are key age-related differences in our moral view of an animal's worth that point to socially constructed development over the lifespan.

BRAIN/COGNITION

Brain-wide mapping reveals that engrams for a single memory are distributed across multiple brain regions

Roy, D. S., Park, Y. G., Kim, M. E., Zhang, Y., Ogawa, S. K., DiNapoli, N., . . . Tonegawa, S. (2022). Brain-wide mapping reveals that engrams for a single memory are distributed across multiple brain regions. *Nature Communications, 13*(1), 1–16. doi:10.1038/s41467-022-29384-4

Abstract
Neuronal ensembles that hold specific memory (memory engrams) have been identified in the hippocampus, amygdala, or cortex. However, it has been hypothesized that engrams of a specific memory are distributed among multiple brain regions that are functionally connected, referred to as a unified engram complex. Here, we report a partial map of the engram complex for contextual fear conditioning memory by characterizing encoding activated neuronal ensembles in 247 regions using tissue phenotyping in mice. The mapping was aided by an engram index, which identified 117 $cFos^+$ brain regions holding engrams with high probability, and brain-wide reactivation of these neuronal ensembles by recall. Optogenetic manipulation experiments revealed engram ensembles, many of which were functionally connected to hippocampal or amygdala engrams. Simultaneous chemogenetic reactivation of multiple engram ensembles conferred a greater level of memory recall than reactivation of a single engram ensemble, reflecting the natural memory recall process. Overall, our study supports the unified engram complex hypothesis for memory storage.

MEF2 is a key regulator of cognitive potential and confers resilience to neurodegeneration

Barker, S. J., Raju, R. M., Milman, N. E., Wang, J., Davila-Velderrain, J., Gunter-Rahman, F., . . . Tsai, L. H. (2021). MEF2 is a key regulator of cognitive potential and confers resilience to neurodegeneration. *Science Translational Medicine, 13*(618), eabd7695. doi:10.1126/scitranslmed.abd7695

Abstract
Recent increases in human longevity have been accompanied by a rise in the incidence of dementia, highlighting the need to preserve cognitive function in an aging population. A small percentage of individuals with pathological hallmarks of neurodegenerative disease are able to maintain normal cognition. Although the molecular mechanisms that govern this neuroprotection remain unknown, individuals that exhibit cognitive resilience (CgR) represent

a unique source of therapeutic insight. For both humans and animal models, living in an enriched, cognitively stimulating environment is the most effective known inducer of CgR. To understand potential drivers of this phenomenon, we began by profiling the molecular changes that arise from environmental enrichment in mice, which led to the identification of MEF2 transcription factors (TFs). We next turned to repositories of human clinical and brain transcriptomic data, where we found that the MEF2 transcriptional network was overrepresented among genes that are most predictive of end-stage cognition. Through single-nucleus RNA sequencing of cortical tissue from resilient and nonresilient individuals, we further confirmed upregulation of MEF2C in resilient individuals to a subpopulation of excitatory neurons. Last, to determine the causal impact of MEF2 on cognition in the context of neurodegeneration, we overexpressed *Mef2a/c* in the PS19 mouse model of tauopathy and found that this was sufficient to improve cognitive flexibility and reduce hyperexcitability. Overall, our findings reveal a previously unappreciated role for MEF2 TFs in promoting CgR, highlighting their potential as biomarkers or therapeutic targets for neurodegeneration and healthy aging.

Factors influencing attenuating skill decay in high-risk industries: A scoping review

Klostermann, M., Conein, S., Felkl, T., & Kluge, A. (2022). Factors influencing attenuating skill decay in high-risk industries: A scoping review. *Safety, 8*(2), 22. doi:10.3390/safety8020022

Abstract

The infrequent use of skills relevant in non-routine situations in highly automated and high-risk industries is a major safety issue. The infrequent use of skills can lead to skill decay. Research on skill decay has a long history, but not much is known about the relevant factors and refresher interventions to attenuate skill decay in highly automated environments. In the present study, a scoping review was conducted to determine whether the well-known factors in skill decay research are also relevant for complex cognitive skill decay and to identify refresher interventions that are deemed effective for attenuating decay. A scoping review aims at identifying, summarizing, and mapping the body of literature on a given topic. Searches in electronic databases, including PsycArticles, PsyINFO, and Psyndex, via EBSCOhost and Web of Science and Google Scholar were conducted, and documents were analyzed regarding the research question, which resulted in $n = 58$ studies. The findings demonstrate the relevance of task characteristics and method-related (cognitive-based, behavioral-based training) and person-related factors (e.g., cognitive ability, experience, motivation) to mitigate decay. Additionally, the results demonstrate that minor refresher interventions are effective at attenuating complex cognitive skill decay. Implications for industry and training providers that aim to implement training and refresher interventions to attenuate skill decay in high-risk industries are provided. Researchers may use the information about the influences of person- and method-related factors, task characteristics, and refresher interventions presented in this scoping review as a starting point to conduct further empirical research by taking skill acquisition, retention, and transfer into account.

Reading on a smartphone affects sigh generation, brain activity, and comprehension

Honma, M., Masaoka, Y., Iizuka, N., Wada, S., Kamimura, S., Yoshikawa, A., . . . Izumizaki, M. (2022). Reading on a smartphone affects sigh generation, brain activity, and comprehension. *Scientific Reports, 12*(1), 1589. doi:10.1038/s41598-022-05605-0

Abstract

Electronic devices have become an indispensable part of our daily lives, while their negative aspects have been reported. One disadvantage is that reading comprehension is reduced when reading from an electronic device; the cause of this deficit in performance is unclear. In this study, we investigated the cause for comprehension decline when reading on a smartphone by simultaneously measuring respiration and brain activity during reading in 34 healthy individuals. We found that, compared to reading on a paper medium, reading on a smartphone elicits fewer sighs, promotes brain overactivity in the prefrontal cortex, and results in reduced comprehension. Furthermore, reading on a smartphone affected sigh frequency but not normal breathing, suggesting that normal breathing and sigh generation are mediated by pathways differentially influenced by the visual environment. A path analysis suggests that the interactive relationship between sigh inhibition and overactivity in the prefrontal cortex causes comprehension decline. These findings provide new insight into the respiration-mediated mechanisms of cognitive function.

Subcortical brain development in autism and fragile X syndrome: Evidence for dynamic, age- and disorder-specific trajectories in infancy

Shen, M. D., Swanson, M. R., Wolff, J. J., Elison, J. T., Girault, J. B., Kim, S. H., . . . IBIS Network. (2022). Subcortical brain development in autism and fragile X syndrome: Evidence for dynamic, age- and disorder-specific trajectories in infancy. *American Journal of Psychiatry.* Advance online publication. doi:10.1176/appi.ajp.21090896

Abstract

Objective: Previous research has demonstrated that the amygdala is enlarged in children with autism spectrum disorder (ASD). However, the precise onset of this enlargement during infancy, how it relates to later diagnostic behaviors, whether the timing of enlargement in infancy is specific to the amygdala, and whether it is specific to ASD (or present in other neurodevelopmental disorders, such as fragile X syndrome) are all unknown.

Methods: Longitudinal MRIs were acquired at 6–24 months of age in 29 infants with fragile X syndrome, 58 infants at high likelihood for ASD who were later diagnosed with ASD, 212 high-likelihood infants not diagnosed with ASD, and 109 control infants (1,099 total scans).

Results: Infants who developed ASD had typically sized amygdala volumes at 6 months, but exhibited significantly faster amygdala growth between 6 and 24 months, such that by 12 months the ASD group had significantly larger amygdala volume (Cohen's $d = .56$) compared with all other groups. Amygdala growth rate between 6 and 12 months was significantly associated with greater social deficits at 24 months when the infants were diagnosed with ASD. Infants with fragile X syndrome had a persistent and significantly enlarged caudate volume at all ages between 6 and 24 months ($d = 2.12$), compared with all other groups, which was significantly associated with greater repetitive behaviors.

Conclusions: This is the first MRI study comparing fragile X syndrome and ASD in infancy, demonstrating strikingly different patterns of brain and behavior development. Fragile X syndrome–related changes were present from 6 months of age, whereas ASD-related changes unfolded over the first 2 years of life, starting with no detectable group differences at 6 months. Increased amygdala growth rate between 6 and 12 months occurs prior to social deficits and well before diagnosis. This gradual onset of brain and behavior changes in ASD, but not fragile X syndrome, suggests an age- and disorder-specific pattern of cascading brain changes preceding autism diagnosis.

Composition within and between languages in the bilingual mind: MEG evidence from Korean/English bilinguals

Phillips, S. F., & Pylkkänen, L. (2021). Composition within and between languages in the bilingual mind: MEG evidence from Korean/English bilinguals. *eNeuro, 8*(6). doi:10.1523/ENEURO.0084-21.2021

Abstract

The ability of the human brain to build complex expressions from simpler parts is fascinating, but the ability of the bilingual brain to do so is perhaps even more remarkable. When highly proficient bilinguals converse, they can fluidly switch from one language to another even inside sentences. Thus, they build expressions using words from more than one language. How are bilinguals able to compose words across different languages in real time? While robust evidence has implicated the left anterior temporal lobe (LATL) for the composition of words within one language, we do not know how the LATL, or other regions implicated for composition, operates when the language switches. We also do not know whether prefrontal regions associated with language control are recruited for language switching during composition. We addressed these questions with magnetoencephalography (MEG) measurements in bilinguals who are fluent in two typologically distant languages, English and Korean. We observed early composition effects in the LATL at ~200 ms that were unaffected by either language or orthography switching, which was also varied (Hangul vs Roman alphabet). Thus, the combinatory mechanism at 200 ms housed in the anterior temporal cortex appears blind to the language in which its input concepts are expressed. However, in later time windows, language and orthography switching interacted both in regions implicated for composition (LATL, ventromedial prefrontal cortex, left inferior frontal gyrus [LIFG]) as well as in regions associated with language control (ACC, LIFG). This establishes a starting point for understanding how bilingual brains code switch: words are initially combined without consideration of which language they come from, but language switching affects later processing.

This is your brain in meltdown

Arnsten, A., Mazure, C. M., & Sinha, R. (2012). This is your brain in meltdown. *Scientific American, 306*(4), 48–53. doi:10.1038/scientificamerican0412-48

Abstract

The entrance exam to medical school consists of a five-hour fusillade of hundreds of questions that, even with the best preparation, often leaves the test taker discombobulated and anxious. For some would-be physicians, the relentless pressure causes their reasoning abilities to slow and even shut down entirely. The experience—known variously as choking, brain freeze, nerves, jitters, folding, blanking out, the yips, or a dozen other descriptive terms—is all too familiar to virtually anyone who has flubbed a speech, bumped up against writer's block, or struggled through a lengthy exam.

For decades scientists thought they understood what happens in the brain during testing or a battlefront firefight. In recent years a different line of research has put the physiology of stress in an entirely new perspective. The response to stress is not just a primal reaction affecting parts of the brain that are common to a wide array of species ranging from salamanders to humans. Stress, in fact, can cripple our most advanced mental faculties, the areas of the brain most developed in primates.

Older textbooks explained that the hypothalamus, an evolutionarily ancient structure lodged at the base of the brain, reacts to stress by triggering the secretion of a wave of hormones from the pituitary and adrenal glands, which makes the heart race, elevates blood pressure, and diminishes appetite. Now research reveals an unexpected role for the prefrontal cortex, the area immediately behind the forehead that serves as the control center that mediates our highest cognitive abilities—among them concentration, planning, decision making, insight, judgment, and the ability to retrieve memories. The prefrontal cortex is the part of the brain that evolved most recently, and it can be exquisitely sensitive to even temporary everyday anxieties and worries.

When things are going well, the prefrontal cortex acts as a control center that keeps our baser emotions and impulses in check. The new research demonstrates that acute, uncontrollable stress sets off a series of chemical events that weaken the influence of the prefrontal cortex while strengthening the dominance of older parts of the brain. In essence, it transfers high-level control over thought and emotion from the prefrontal cortex to the hypothalamus and other earlier evolved structures. As the older parts take over, we may find ourselves either consumed by paralyzing anxiety or else subject to impulses that we usually manage to keep in check: indulgence in excesses of food, drink, drugs, or a spending spree at a local specialty store. Quite simply, we lose it.

The growing understanding that acute stress can severely compromise the function of higher "executive" areas in the human brain has drawn the interest of investigators. They are now not just trying to understand what happens in your head when you freeze but also developing behavioral and pharmaceutical interventions to help you keep your composure.

Sniffing submissiveness? Oxytocin administration in severe psychopathy

Rijnders, R. J., Dykstra, A. H., Terburg, D., Kempes, M. M., & van Honk, J. (2021). Sniffing submissiveness? Oxytocin administration in severe psychopathy. *Psychoneuroendocrinology, 131,* 105330. doi:10.1016/j.psyneuen.2021.105330

Abstract

Psychopathy is a personality disorder associated with criminal behavior and violent recidivism, and therefore a burden to society. Social dominance is one of the characteristics of psychopathy that might contribute to these problems. Nevertheless, only few studies have objectively measured the relationship between socially dominant behavior and psychopathy. Therefore, the current study assessed performance of 21 forensic PCL-R confirmed psychopathic patients and 24 normal controls on a gaze aversion task, in which slower gaze aversion from masked angry faces compared to masked happy faces is a measure of reactive dominance. Moreover, the current study assessed the potential beneficial effects of the neuropeptide oxytocin. The results showed that psychopaths were not more dominant on the gaze aversion task compared to normal controls. However, the severity of psychopathy was positively correlated with reactive dominance. Crucially, a single nasal spray administration of oxytocin abolished the connection between psychopathy and reactive dominance. This implies that socially dominant psychopaths might benefit from oxytocin administration.

Medial prefrontal and occipito-temporal activity at encoding determines enhanced recognition of threatening faces after 1.5 years

Liu, X., Zhou, X., Zeng, Y., Li, J., Zhao, W., Xu, L., . . . Becker, B. (2022). Medial prefrontal and occipito-temporal activity at encoding determines enhanced recognition of threatening faces after 1.5 years. *Brain Structure and Function,* 1–18. doi:10.1007/s00429-022-02462-5

Abstract

Studies demonstrated that faces with threatening emotional expressions are better remembered than non-threatening faces. However, whether this memory advantage persists over years and which neural systems underlie such an effect remains unknown. Here, we employed an individual difference approach to examine whether the neural activity during incidental encoding was associated with differential recognition of faces with emotional expressions (angry, fearful, happy, sad, and neutral) after a retention interval of > 1.5 years ($N = 89$). Behaviorally, we found a better recognition for threatening (angry, fearful) versus non-threatening (happy and neutral) faces after a delay of > 1.5 years, which was driven by forgetting of non-threatening faces compared with immediate recognition after encoding. Multivariate principal component analysis (PCA) on the behavioral responses further confirmed the discriminative recognition performance between threatening and non-threatening faces. A voxel-wise whole-brain analysis on the concomitantly acquired functional magnetic resonance imaging (fMRI) data during incidental encoding revealed that neural activity in bilateral inferior occipital gyrus (IOG) and ventromedial prefrontal/orbitofrontal cortex (vmPFC/OFC) was associated with the individual differences in the discriminative emotional face recognition performance measured by an innovative behavioral pattern similarity analysis (BPSA). The left fusiform face area (FFA) was additionally determined using a regionally focused analysis. Overall, the present study provides evidence that threatening facial expressions lead to persistent face recognition over periods of > 1.5 years, and that differential encoding-related activity in the medial prefrontal cortex and occipito-temporal cortex may underlie this effect.

The hippocampus and orbitofrontal cortex jointly represent task structure during memory-guided decision making

Mızrak, E., Bouffard, N. R., Libby, L. A., Boorman, E. D., & Ranganath, C. (2021). The hippocampus and orbitofrontal cortex jointly represent task structure during memory-guided decision making. *Cell Reports, 37*(9), 110065. doi:10.1016/j.celrep.2021.110065

Abstract

The hippocampus, well known for its role in episodic memory, might also be an important brain region for extracting structure from our experiences in order to guide future decisions. Recent evidence in rodents suggests that the hippocampus supports decision making by representing task structure in cooperation with the orbitofrontal cortex (OFC). Here, we examine how the human hippocampus and OFC represent task structure during an associative learning task that required learning of both context-determined and context-invariant probabilistic associations. We find that after learning, hippocampal and lateral OFC representations differentiated between context-determined and context-invariant task structures. The degree of this differentiation within the hippocampus and lateral OFC is highly correlated. These results advance our understanding of the hippocampus and suggest that the hippocampus and OFC support goal-directed behavior by representing information that guides the selection of appropriate decision strategies.

Examining the effects of goal-setting, feedback, and incentives on sustained attention

Robison, M. K., Unsworth, N., & Brewer, G. A. (2021). Examining the effects of goal-setting, feedback, and incentives on sustained attention. *Journal of Experimental Psychology: Human Perception and Performance, 47*(6), 869. doi:10.1037/xhp0000926

Abstract

Across four experiments, we examined the effects of goal-setting, feedback, and incentivizing manipulations on sustained attention. In addition to measuring task performance, we measured subjective attentional states and momentary feelings of motivation and alertness. Experiment 1 compared two specific goal conditions—one difficult and one easy—with a standard set of instructions. The specific goal conditions both reduced RTs and attenuated the vigilance decrement but did not impact task engagement (motivation or task-unrelated thoughts). Experiment 2 manipulated both goal-setting and feedback across conditions. The combination of a specific goal and feedback had strong effects on both task performance and task engagement. Additionally, feedback increased task engagement (higher motivation and fewer task-unrelated thoughts) regardless of whether or not it was paired with a specific goal. Experiment 3 examined the effect of pairing goals with a reward. Participants in one reward condition (time-based incentive) reported higher motivation but did not show better task performance. Offering a cash incentive to meet a goal did not have an effect on any dependent variables. Finally, in an effort to examine whether more moderately difficult goals might lead to optimal performance, Experiment 4 examined a broader range of goals. However, we did not see an effect of a moderately difficult goal on any of the dependent variables. Although some of the experimental manipulations were effective in mitigating the vigilance decrement, none eliminated it. We discuss the theoretical implications of the results with regard to goal-setting theory and theories of vigilance.

Spaced training enhances memory and prefrontal ensemble stability in mice

Glas, A., Hübener, M., Bonhoeffer, T., & Goltstein, P. M. (2021). Spaced training enhances memory and prefrontal ensemble stability in mice. *Current Biology, 31*(18), 4052–4061. doi:10.1016/j.cub.2021.06.085

Abstract

It is commonly acknowledged that memory is substantially improved when learning is distributed over time, an effect called the "spacing effect." So far it has not been studied how spaced learning affects the neuronal ensembles presumably underlying memory. In the present study, we investigate whether trial spacing increases the stability or size of neuronal ensembles. Mice were trained in the "everyday memory" task, an appetitive, naturalistic, delayed matching-to-place task. Spacing trials by 60 minutes produced more robust memories than training with shorter or longer intervals. c-Fos labeling and chemogenetic inactivation established the involvement of the dorsomedial prefrontal cortex (dmPFC) in successful memory storage. In vivo calcium imaging of excitatory dmPFC neurons revealed that longer trial spacing increased the similarity of the population activity pattern on subsequent encoding trials and upon retrieval. Conversely, trial spacing did not affect the size of the total neuronal ensemble or the size of subpopulations dedicated to specific task-related behaviors and events. Thus, spaced learning promotes reactivation of prefrontal neuronal ensembles processing episodic-like memories.

Team flow is a unique brain state associated with enhanced information integration and interbrain synchrony

Shehata, M., Cheng, M., Leung, A., Tsuchiya, N., Wu, D. A., Tseng, C. H., . . . Shimojo, S. (2021). Team flow is a unique brain state associated with enhanced information integration and interbrain synchrony. *eNeuro, 8*(5). doi:10.1523/ENEURO.0133-21.2021

Abstract

Team flow occurs when a group functions in a high task engagement to achieve a goal, commonly seen in performance and sports. Team flow can enable enhanced positive experiences, as compared with individual flow or regular socializing. However, the neural basis for this enhanced behavioral state remains unclear. Here, we identified neural correlates (NCs) of team flow in human participants using a music rhythm task with electroencephalogram hyper-scanning. Experimental manipulations held the motor task constant while disrupting the corresponding hedonic music to interfere with the flow state or occluding the partner's positive feedback to impede team interaction. We validated these manipulations by using psychometric ratings and an objective measure for the depth of flow experience, which uses the auditory-evoked potential (AEP) of a task-irrelevant stimulus. Spectral power analysis at both the scalp sensors and anatomic source levels revealed higher β-γ power specific to team flow in the left middle temporal cortex (L-MTC). Causal interaction analysis revealed that the L-MTC is downstream in information processing and receives information from areas encoding the flow or social states. The L-MTC significantly contributes to integrating information. Moreover, we found that team flow enhances global interbrain integrated information (II) and neural synchrony. We conclude that the NCs of team flow induce a distinct brain state. Our results suggest a neurocognitive mechanism to create this unique experience.

Neural representations of the committed romantic partner in the nucleus accumbens

Ueda, R., & Abe, N. (2021). Neural representations of the committed romantic partner in the nucleus accumbens. *Psychological Science, 32*(12), 1884–1895. doi:10.1177/09567976211021854

Abstract
Having an intimate romantic relationship is an important aspect of life. Dopamine-rich reward regions, including the nucleus accumbens (NAcc), have been identified as neural correlates for both emotional bonding with the partner and interest in unfamiliar attractive nonpartners. Here, we aimed to disentangle the overlapping functions of the NAcc using multivoxel pattern analysis, which can decode the cognitive processes encoded in particular neural activity. During functional MRI scanning, 46 romantically involved men performed the social-incentive-delay task, in which a successful response resulted in the presentation of a dynamic and positive facial expression from their partner and unfamiliar women. Multivoxel pattern analysis revealed that the spatial patterns of NAcc activity could successfully discriminate between romantic partners and unfamiliar women during the period in which participants anticipated the target presentation. We speculate that neural activity patterns within the NAcc represent the relationship partner, which might be a key neural mechanism for committed romantic relationships.

Healthy or not? The impact of conflicting health-related information on attentional resources

Barnwell, P. V., Fedorenko, E. J., & Contrada, R. J. (2022). Healthy or not? The impact of conflicting health-related information on attentional resources. *Journal of Behavioral Medicine, 45*(2), 306–317. doi:10.1007/s10865-021-00256-4

Abstract
Despite its ubiquity, little is known about the impact of exposure to conflicting health information on cognitive efficiency. We hypothesized that it would reduce attentional capacity, as evidenced by (1) increased response errors during the Attention Network Test (ANT), (2) decreased efficiency of each ANT system (alerting, orienting, execute control), and (3) increased self-reported workload, (4) nutritional confusion, and (5) nutritional backlash. A sample of 184 online participants was used, assigned randomly to read an article containing either congruent or conflicting health information. Subsequently, they completed the ANT and self-report measures of workload, nutritional confusion, and backlash at nutritional recommendations and research. Participants in the conflicting health information condition made more errors, had overall slower reaction times, and reported greater workload, nutritional confusion, and backlash. No differences were found for individual ANT systems. These findings suggest that exposure to conflicting health information can degrade attentional mechanisms responsible for accurate and prompt responding to incoming information.

COVID

EFT (Emotional Freedom Technique) as an alternative therapy to reduce anxiety disorders and depression in people who are positive Covid-19

Tambunan, M. B., Suwarni, L., Setiawati, L., & Mardjan, M. (2022). EFT (Emotional Freedom Technique) as an alternative therapy to reduce anxiety disorders and depression in people who are positive Covid-19. *Psikostudia: Jurnal Psikologi, 11*(1), 59–68. doi:10.30872/psikostudia

Abstract

The increasing number of deaths from COVID-19 is in line with anxiety disorders and depression in people who are positive for COVID-19. The emotional Freedom Technique (EFT) is known as an effective therapy to reduce mental health disorders in certain patients but has never been applied to people who are confirmed positive for COVID-19. This study aims to analyze the effectiveness of EFT as an alternative therapy in reducing anxiety and depression in people who are positive for COVID-19. This research design uses a quasi-experimental approach with a one-group pretest and posttest approach. A total of 22 people were isolated in the Health Training Unit (UPELKES) provided by the Pontianak Government of Indonesia in June 2021. The data analysis technique used paired t-test (95% CI). There was a significant decrease in anxiety ($t = 6{,}738$) and depression scores ($t = 2{,}585$) after EFT therapy was given ($p < .05$). Thus, EFT can be an alternative therapy in overcoming anxiety and depression disorders in people who are confirmed positive for COVID-19.

Psychological effects of online-based mindfulness programs during the COVID-19 pandemic: A systematic review of randomized controlled trials

Yeun, Y. R., & Kim, S. D. (2022). Psychological effects of online-based mindfulness programs during the COVID-19 pandemic: A systematic review of randomized controlled trials. *International Journal of Environmental Research and Public Health, 19*(3), 1624. doi:10.3390/ijerph19031624

Abstract

Background: The COVID-19 outbreak has caused psychological problems worldwide. This review explored the psychological effects of online-based mindfulness programs during the COVID-19 pandemic.

Methods: This systematic review was guided by the Preferred Reporting Items for Systematic Reviews and Meta-Analyses guidelines. Randomized controlled trials that were published in the English language from January 1, 2020 to May 31, 2021 on online-based mindfulness programs for psychological problems due to the COVID-19 pandemic were searched in electronic databases. Quality assessment was conducted on the retrieved RCTs using the Cochrane risk of bias tool for RCTs.

Results: Six RCTs were included in this review. Quality appraisal of included RCTs ranged from 1 for low risk of bias to 5 for high risk of bias. There is evidence from the six RCTs that online-based mindfulness interventions may have favorable effects for reducing the levels of psychological problems, such as anxiety, depression, and stress.

Conclusions: Online-based mindfulness programs may be used as complementary interventions for clinical populations, healthy individuals, and healthcare workers with psychological problems due to the COVID-19 pandemic.

[*Note from the editors:* One of the RCTs studied EFT. Yeun and Kim stated of this RCT, "Interestingly, tapping practice as an emotional freedom technique showed a significant decline in the level of anxiety and stress in the trained group compared to the control group, which can be evaluated as evidence for a reduction in anxiety and stress levels in nurses caring for COVID-19 patients."]

Short-term and long-term rates of postacute sequelae of SARS-CoV-2 infection: A systematic review

Groff, D., Sun, A., Ssentongo, A. E., Ba, D. M., Parsons, N., Poudel, G. R., . . . Chinchilli, V. M. (2021). Short-term and long-term rates of postacute sequelae of SARS-CoV-2 infection: A systematic review. *JAMA Network Open, 4*(10), e2128568. doi:10.1001/jamanetworkopen.2021.28568

Abstract

Importance: Short-term and long-term persistent postacute sequelae of COVID-19 (PASC) have not been systematically evaluated. The incidence and evolution of PASC are dependent on time from infection, organ systems and tissue affected, vaccination status, variant of the virus, and geographic region.

Objective: To estimate organ system–specific frequency and evolution of PASC.

Evidence review: PubMed (MEDLINE), Scopus, the World Health Organization Global Literature on Coronavirus Disease, and CoronaCentral databases were searched from December 2019 through March 2021. A total of 2,100 studies were identified from databases and through cited references. Studies providing data on PASC in children and adults were included. The Preferred Reporting Items for Systematic Reviews and Meta-analyses (PRISMA) guidelines for abstracting data were followed and performed independently by two reviewers. Quality was assessed using the Newcastle-Ottawa Scale for cohort studies. The main outcome was frequency of PASC diagnosed by (1) laboratory investigation, (2) radiologic pathology, and (3) clinical signs and symptoms. PASC were classified by organ system (i.e., neurologic, cardiovascular, respiratory, digestive, dermatologic, and ear, nose, and throat) as well as mental health, constitutional symptoms, and functional mobility.

Findings: From a total of 2,100 studies identified, 57 studies with 250,351 survivors of COVID-19 met inclusion criteria. The mean (SD) age of survivors was 54.4 (8.9) years, 140,196 (56%) were male, and 197,777 (79%) were hospitalized during acute COVID-19. High-income countries contributed 45 studies (79%). The median (IQR) proportion of COVID-19 survivors experiencing at least one PASC was 54.0% (45.0%–69.0%; 13 studies) at 1 month (short-term), 55.0% (34.8%–65.5%; 38 studies) at 2 to 5 months (intermediate-term), and 54.0% (31.0%–67.0%; 9 studies) at 6 or more months (long-term). Most prevalent pulmonary sequelae, neurologic disorders, mental health disorders, functional mobility impairments, and general and constitutional symptoms were chest imaging abnormality (median [IQR], 62.2% [45.8%–76.5%]), difficulty concentrating (median [IQR], 23.8% [20.4%–25.9%]), generalized anxiety disorder (median [IQR], 29.6% [14.0%–44.0%]), general functional impairments (median [IQR], 44.0% [23.4%–62.6%]), and fatigue or muscle weakness (median [IQR], 37.5% [25.4%–54.5%]), respectively. Other frequently reported symptoms included cardiac, dermatologic, digestive, and ear, nose, and throat disorders.

Conclusions and relevance: In this systematic review, more than half of COVID-19 survivors experienced PASC six months after recovery. The most common PASC involved functional mobility impairments, pulmonary abnormalities, and mental health disorders. These long-term PASC effects occur on a scale that could overwhelm existing health care capacity, particularly in low- and middle-income countries.

Don't put all social network sites in one basket: Facebook, Instagram, Twitter, TikTok, and their relations with well-being during the COVID-19 pandemic

Masciantonio, A., Bourguignon, D., Bouchat, P., Balty, M., & Rimé, B. (2021). Don't put all social network sites in one basket: Facebook, Instagram, Twitter, TikTok, and their relations with well-being during the COVID-19 pandemic. *PloS One, 16*(3), e0248384. doi:10.1371/journal.pone.0248384

Abstract

Prior studies indicated that actively using social network sites (SNSs) is positively associated with well-being by enhancing social support and feelings of connectedness. Conversely, passively using SNSs is negatively associated with well-being by fostering upward social comparison and envy. However, the majority of these studies has focused on Facebook. The present research examined the relationships between well-being—satisfaction with life, negative affect, positive affect—and using actively or passively various SNSs—Facebook, Instagram, Twitter, TikTok—during the COVID-19 pandemic. In addition, two mediators were tested: social support and upward social comparison. One thousand four persons completed an online survey during the quarantine measures; the analyses employed structural equation modeling. Results showed that passive usage of Facebook is negatively related to well-being through upward social comparison, whereas active usage of Instagram is positively related to satisfaction with life and negative affect through social support. Furthermore, active usage of Twitter was positively related to satisfaction with life through social support; while passive usage was negatively related to upward social comparison, which, in turn, was associated with more negative affect. Finally, TikTok use was not associated with well-being. Results are discussed in line with SNSs' architectures and users' motivations. Future research is required to go beyond methodological and statistical limitations and allow generalization. This study concludes that SNSs must be differentiated to truly understand how they shape human interactions.

SARS-CoV-2 is associated with changes in brain structure in UK Biobank

Douaud, G., Lee, S., Alfaro-Almagro, F., Arthofer, C., Wang, C., McCarthy, P., . . . Smith, S. M. (2022). SARS-CoV-2 is associated with changes in brain structure in UK Biobank. *Nature,* 1–17. doi:10.1101/2021.06.11.21258690

Abstract

There is strong evidence for brain-related abnormalities in COVID-19. It remains unknown, however, whether the impact of SARS-CoV-2 infection can be detected in milder cases, and whether this can reveal possible mechanisms contributing to brain pathology. Here, we investigated brain changes in 785 UK Biobank participants (aged 51–81) imaged twice, including 401 cases who tested positive for infection with SARS-CoV-2 between their two scans, with 141 days on average separating their diagnosis and second scan, and 384 controls. The availability of preinfection imaging data reduces the likelihood of preexisting risk factors being misinterpreted as disease effects. We identified significant longitudinal effects when comparing the two groups, including: (i) greater reduction in grey matter thickness and tissue-contrast in the orbitofrontal cortex and parahippocampal gyrus, (ii) greater changes in markers of tissue damage in regions functionally connected to the primary olfactory cortex, and (iii) greater reduction in global brain size. The infected participants also showed on average larger cognitive decline between the two time points. Importantly, these imaging and cognitive longitudinal effects were still seen after excluding the 15 cases who had been hospitalized. These mainly limbic brain imaging results may be the in vivo hallmarks of a degenerative spread of the disease via olfactory pathways, of neuroinflammatory events, or of the loss of sensory input due to anosmia. Whether this deleterious impact can be partially reversed, or whether these effects will persist in the long term, remains to be investigated with additional follow-up.

When intelligence hurts and ignorance is bliss: Global pandemic as an evolutionarily novel threat to happiness

Kanazawa, S., Li, N. P., & Yong, J. C. (2022). When intelligence hurts and ignorance is bliss: Global pandemic as an evolutionarily novel threat to happiness. *Journal of Personality.* Advance online publication. doi:10.1111/jopy.12709

Abstract

Introduction: The savanna theory of happiness posits that it is not only the current consequences of a given situation that affect happiness but also its ancestral consequences, and that the effect of ancestral consequences on happiness is stronger among less intelligent individuals. But what about situations that did not exist in the ancestral environment and thus have no ancestral consequences? Global pandemic is one such situation that has no ancestral analog, and the theory predicts such evolutionarily novel threats to have a negative effect disproportionately on the life satisfaction of more intelligent individuals.

Methods: We analyzed prospectively longitudinal data from population samples from the National Child Development Study (Study 1) and the British Cohort Study (Study 2).

Results: Consistent with the theoretical prediction, while more intelligent individuals were generally more satisfied with their lives than less intelligent individuals were throughout adulthood (albeit not because they were more intelligent but because they earned more money, were more likely to be married, and healthier), more intelligent individuals were less satisfied with their lives during the COVID-19 global pandemic because they were more intelligent.

Conclusion: Higher intelligence may have a downside in the modern world, by allowing life satisfaction to be more vulnerable from being better able to comprehend the severity of problems that did not exist in the ancestral world.

GRATITUDE/WELL-BEING

The cultivation of pure altruism via gratitude: A functional MRI study of change with gratitude practice

Karns, C. M., Moore III, W. E., & Mayr, U. (2017). The cultivation of pure altruism via gratitude: A functional MRI study of change with gratitude practice. *Frontiers in Human Neuroscience, 11,* 599. doi:10.3389/fnhum.2017.00599

Abstract
Gratitude is an emotion and a trait linked to well-being and better health, and welcoming benefits to oneself is instrumentally valuable. However, theoretical and empirical work highlights that gratitude is more fully understood as an intrinsically valuable moral emotion. To understand the role of neural reward systems in the association between gratitude and altruistic motivations, we tested two hypotheses. First, whether self-reported propensity toward gratitude relates to fMRI-derived indicators of "pure altruism," operationalized as the neural valuation of passive, private transfers to a charity versus to oneself. In young adult female participants, self-reported gratitude and altruism were associated with "neural pure altruism" in ventromedial prefrontal cortex (VMPFC) and nucleus accumbens. Second, whether neural pure altruism can be increased through practicing gratitude. In a double-blind study, we randomly assigned participants to either a gratitude-journal or active-neutral control journal group for three weeks. Relative to pretest levels, gratitude journaling increased the neural pure altruism response in the VMPFC. We posit that as a context-dependent value-sensitive cortical region, the VMPFC supports change with gratitude practice, a change that is larger for benefits to others versus oneself.

Letters of gratitude: Further evidence for author benefits

Toepfer, S. M., Cichy, K., & Peters, P. (2012). Letters of gratitude: Further evidence for author benefits. *Journal of Happiness Studies: An Interdisciplinary Forum on Subjective Well-Being, 13*(1), 187–201. doi:10.1007/s10902-011-9257-7

Abstract
This study examined the effects of writing letters of gratitude on three primary qualities of well-being: happiness (positive affect), life satisfaction (cognitive evaluation), and depression (negative affect). Gratitude was also assessed. Participants included 219 men and women who wrote three letters of gratitude over a three-week period. A two-way mixed method ANOVA with a between factor (writers vs. non-writers) and within subject factor (time of testing) analysis was conducted. Results indicated that writing letters of gratitude increased participants' happiness and life satisfaction, while decreasing depressive symptoms. The implications of this approach for intervention are discussed.

How a gratitude intervention influences workplace mistreatment: A multiple mediation model

Locklear, L. R., Taylor, S. G., & Ambrose, M. L. (2021). How a gratitude intervention influences workplace mistreatment: A multiple mediation model. *Journal of Applied Psychology, 106*(9), 1314. doi:10.1037/apl0000825

Abstract

Despite wide-ranging negative consequences of interpersonal mistreatment, research offers few practical solutions to reduce such behavior in organizations. Given that interpersonal relationships are strengthened and desired employee behaviors are more frequent when individuals purposefully cultivate feelings of gratitude, the present study tests the effectiveness of a 10-day gratitude journaling intervention in reducing workplace incivility, gossip, and ostracism. Because research has not examined the mechanisms by which gratitude interventions influence outcomes, we draw on theory and research from the gratitude literature to propose and test a multiple mediator model. Specifically, we examine the moral affect theory of gratitude, find-remind-and-bind theory, self-regulation theory, and social exchange theory as possible explanations for the effects of the intervention. Two field experiments involving 147 (Study 1) and 204 (Study 2) employees demonstrated that the intervention decreased mistreatment (as reported by coworkers) by enhancing self-control resources. We also found that the effects of the intervention were stronger for individuals who perceive higher norms for gratitude in their workplace. The findings support the resource-building nature of gratitude interventions and demonstrate that a gratitude intervention is one effective way to decrease interpersonal mistreatment in organizations. Implications for theory and practice are discussed.

It's the little things: Everyday gratitude as a booster shot for romantic relationships

Algoe, S. B., Gable, S. L., & Maisel, N. C. (2010). It's the little things: Everyday gratitude as a booster shot for romantic relationships. *Personal Relationships, 17*(2), 217–233. doi:10.1111/j.1475-6811.2010.01273.x

Abstract

Gratitude and indebtedness are differently valenced emotional responses to benefits provided, which have implications for interpersonal processes. Drawing on a social functional model of emotions, we tested the roles of gratitude and indebtedness in romantic relationships with a daily-experience sampling of both members of cohabiting couples. As hypothesized, the receipt of thoughtful benefits predicted both gratitude and indebtedness. Men had more mixed emotional responses to benefit receipt than women. However, for both men and women, gratitude from interactions predicted increases in relationship connection and satisfaction the following day, for both recipient and benefactor. Although indebtedness may maintain external signals of relationship engagement, gratitude had uniquely predictive power in relationship promotion, perhaps acting as a booster shot for the relationship.

Putting laughter in context: Shared laughter as behavioral indicator of relationship well-being

Kurtz, L. E., & Algoe, S. B. (2015). Putting laughter in context: Shared laughter as behavioral indicator of relationship well-being. *Personal Relationships, 22*(4), 573–590. doi:10.1111/pere.12095

Abstract

Laughter is a pervasive human behavior that most frequently happens in a social context. However, data linking the behavior of laughter with psychological or social outcomes are exceptionally rare. Here, the authors draw attention to shared laughter as a useful objective marker of relationship well-being. Spontaneously generated laughs of 71 heterosexual romantic couples were coded from a videorecorded conversation about how the couple first met. Multilevel models revealed that while controlling for all other laughter present, the proportion of the conversation spent laughing simultaneously with the romantic partner was uniquely positively associated with global evaluations of relationship quality, closeness, and social support. Results are discussed with respect to methodological considerations and theoretical implications for relationships and behavioral research more broadly.

Do grittier people have greater subjective well-being? A meta-analysis

Hou, X. L., Becker, N., Hu, T. Q., Koch, M., Xi, J. Z., & Mõttus, R. (2021). Do grittier people have greater subjective well-being? A meta-analysis. *Personality and Social Psychology Bulletin.* Advance online publication. doi:10.1177/01461672211053453

Abstract

The present study conducted a meta-analysis to examine the relation between grit and subjective well-being (SWB). The association between grit (i.e., overall grit, perseverance of effort, and consistency of interest) and SWB (i.e., positive affect, negative affect, happiness, depression, life satisfaction, job satisfaction, and school satisfaction) were synthesized across 83 studies and 66,518 participants. The results based on a random-effects model showed a substantial correlation between overall grit and SWB (ρ = .46, 95% confidence interval [CI] = [.43, .48]), followed by perseverance of effort (ρ = .38, 95% CI = [.33, .43]) and consistency of interest (ρ = .23, 95% CI = [.17, .28]). The moderator analysis indicated that the correlations between overall grit/consistency of effort and SWB become weaker as age increased, and these links were stronger in affective well-being than in cognitive well-being. Moreover, grit explained unique variance in SWB even after controlling for conscientiousness. Implications and directions for further research are discussed.

The effect of EFT (Emotional Freedom Technique) to the self esteem among nurses

Wati, N. L., Sansuwito, T. B., Rai, R. P., Darmawati, I., Anggareni, R., Amir, M. D., & Nasiatin, T. (2022). The effect of EFT (Emotional Freedom Technique) to the self esteem among nurses. *Malaysian Journal of Medicine and Health Sciences, 18*(Supp 2), 239–242.

Abstract

Introduction: Nurses are imperative providers in helping people within health services, but many have problems with self-esteem. Self-esteem is an essential component in building good mental health. One of the complementary therapies that can help improve mental health is the Emotional Freedom Technique (EFT). EFT, a safe psychological energy therapy, employs tapping on certain body spots while repeating words or affirmations. This study aims to examine the effect of EFT on self-esteem.

Methods: A pre-post test was used in this quasi-experimental investigation. The sampling technique used convenience sampling for 115 participants who joined EFT Training. Self-esteem was measured using the Rosenberg Self-Esteem Scale, which was administered to all participants. It was decided to use the paired *t*-test to determine the mean difference between pre and postintervention.

Results: EFT was effective in increasing self-esteem, with a substantial outcome ($p = .000$).

Conclusion: Emotional Freedom Technique (EFT) can be an alternative intervention for boosting nurses' self-esteem.

First impressions count! The role of the human's emotional state on rapport established with an empathic versus neutral virtual therapist

Ranjbartabar, H., Richards, D., Bilgin, A., & Kutay, C. (2021). First impressions count! The role of the human's emotional state on rapport established with an empathic versus neutral virtual therapist. *IEEE Transactions on Affective Computing, 12*(3), 788–800. doi:10.1109/TAFFC.2019.2899305

Abstract

Intelligent virtual agents are being endowed with empathic behaviors to perform roles such as virtual therapists. Studies often evaluate the level of rapport established but do not measure the therapeutic benefit and the relative advantage of empathic versus neutral behaviors. We have created two virtual (empathic/neutral) therapists. Our experiment with 63 participants consisted of one within-subjects (empathic/neutral) and one between-subjects (order) factors. Regardless of the virtual therapist used, improvements in baseline emotion were reported after the first interaction (time one) and further improvement after the second interaction (time two). Our study reveals that if the human initially expresses strong emotional feeling for a problem they are facing, rapport will be higher for the empathic therapist and the level of rapport established at the first meeting will persist regardless of whether the second encounter used empathic or neutral dialogue. Conversely, participants experiencing low emotional feeling reported greater rapport with the neutral therapist, and that level of rapport persisted in the second encounter with the alternative therapist. This study shows that an empathic agent will not necessarily build more rapport or deliver better emotional outcomes than a neutral agent. Further studies are needed to determine when tailoring and complex behaviors are justified.

A laboratory study comparing the effectiveness of verbal and nonverbal rapport-building techniques in interviews

Novotny, E., Frank, M. G., & Grizzard, M. (2021). A laboratory study comparing the effectiveness of verbal and nonverbal rapport-building techniques in interviews. *Communication Studies, 72*(5), 819–833. doi:10.1080/10510974.2021.1975141

Abstract
The relative and combined effectiveness of verbal versus nonverbal techniques in eliciting rapport during interviews is unknown. The effectiveness of one verbal and one nonverbal behavioral technique presumed to be associated with rapport-building was compared to determine if either or both could influence participants to disclose more personal information. In an experiment, an interviewer performed one of four conditions with participants: verbal commonalities, mirrored body postures, a combination of both, or neither (control). Results indicated that participants were more willing to discuss personal, or "closed" topics, when verbal commonalities were used alone, versus in conjunction with nonverbal mirroring. The simple effect of mirroring trended in the predicted direction but was not significantly different from the control group. Practical and research-based implications for rapport-building in interviews are discussed.

PTSD/TRAUMA

Protocol for individual participant data meta-analysis of interventions for posttraumatic stress

Wright, S., Karyotaki, E., Bisson, J., Cuijpers, P., Papola, D., Witteveen, A., . . . Sijbrandij, M. (2022). Protocol for individual participant data meta-analysis of interventions for posttraumatic stress. *BMJ Open, 12*(2), e054830. doi:10.1136/bmjopen-2021-054830

Abstract
Introduction: Several evidence-based treatments are effective for posttraumatic stress disorder (PTSD), yet a substantial proportion of patients do not respond or drop out of treatment. We describe the protocol for a systematic review and individual participant data meta-analysis (IPD-MA) aimed at assessing the effectiveness and adverse effects of psychotherapy and pharmacotherapy interventions for treating PTSD. Additionally, we seek to examine moderators and predictors of treatment outcomes.

Method and analysis: This IPD-MA includes randomized controlled trials comparing psychotherapy and pharmacotherapy interventions for PTSD. PubMed, Embase, PsycINFO, PTSDpubs, and CENTRAL will be screened up till January 11, 2021. The target population is adults with above-threshold baseline PTSD symptoms on any standardized self-report measure. Trials will only be eligible if at least 70% of the study sample have been diagnosed with PTSD by means of a structured clinical interview. The primary outcomes of this IPD-MA are PTSD symptom severity, and response rate. Secondary outcomes include treatment dropout and adverse effects. Two independent reviewers will screen major bibliographic databases and past reviews. Authors will be contacted to contribute their participant-level datasets. Datasets will be merged into a master dataset. A one-stage IPD-MA will be conducted focusing on the effects of psychological and pharmacological interventions on PTSD symptom severity, response rate, treatment dropout, and adverse effects. Subsequent analyses will focus on examining the effect of moderators and predictors of treatment outcomes. These will include sociodemographic, treatment-related, symptom-related, resilience, intervention, trauma, and combat-related characteristics. By determining the individual factors that influence the effectiveness of specific PTSD treatments, we will gain insight into personalized treatment options for PTSD.

Ethics and dissemination: Specific ethics approval for an IPD-MA is not required as this study entails secondary analysis of existing anonymized data. The results of this study will be published in peer-reviewed scientific journals and presentations.

An observational study on acupuncture for earthquake-related post-traumatic stress disorder: The experience of the Lombard Association of Medical Acupuncturists/ Acupuncture in the World, in Amatrice, central Italy

Moiraghi, C., Poli, P., & Piscitelli, A. (2019). An observational study on acupuncture for earthquake-related post-traumatic stress disorder: The experience of the Lombard Association of Medical Acupuncturists/Acupuncture in the World, in Amatrice, central Italy. *Medical Acupuncture, 31*(2), 116–122. doi:10.1089/acu.2018.1329

Abstract
Background and Objective: Earthquakes are associated with severe psychiatric disorders, such as anxiety, depression, and posttraumatic stress disorder (PTSD). Current first-line therapies for PTSD have well-known side effects. Acupuncture is a complementary approach to help patients cope with mental problems after natural disasters and public health events. This article describes an acupuncture intervention conducted by the Lombard Association of Medical Acupuncturists/Acupuncture in the World in the earthquake-stricken area of Amatrice in Central Italy and measures the effect of acupuncture on earthquake-related pain and psychological symptoms in the victims.

Methods: The intervention lasted five weeks, from September to October 2016. Adult patients with psychological symptoms and musculoskeletal pain were included. Treatments were performed by experienced medical acupuncturists. A verbal/numerical scale was developed to quantify the effect of intervention. A Wilcoxon rank-sum test was used for comparison of the scores before and after the acupuncture treatment.

Results: Of the patients, 68.3% reported having both pain and psychological symptoms. The most frequently used meridian points were Kidney (13.17%), followed by Large Intestine (12.46%), Spleen (12.04%), and Gall Bladder (10.34%). After three treatments performed in daily sessions, 54.05% and 60.6% of patients reported marked improvements in psychological and pain symptoms, respectively. Statistical analysis showed a significant difference between the scores reported before the first treatment and after the third treatment, both for pain ($p = .000$) and psychological symptoms ($p = .000$). No serious adverse events were reported.

Conclusions: These results suggest that acupuncture could be a useful tool for reducing pain and psychological symptoms related to earthquakes, but further research is required in this specific area.

Sleep management in posttraumatic stress disorder: A systematic review and meta-analysis

Maher, A. R., Apaydin, E. A., Hilton, L., Chen, C., Troxel, W., Hall, O., . . . Hempel, S. (2021). Sleep management in posttraumatic stress disorder: A systematic review and meta-analysis. *Sleep Medicine, 87,* 203–219. doi:10.1016/j.sleep.2021.08.016

Abstract
Objective: Posttraumatic stress disorder (PTSD) can lead to many negative secondary outcomes for patients, including sleep disturbances. The objective of this meta-analysis is (1) to evaluate the effect of interventions for adults with PTSD on sleep outcomes, PTSD outcomes, and adverse events, and (2) to evaluate the differential effectiveness of interventions aiming to improve sleep compared to those that do not.

Methods: Nine databases were searched for relevant randomized controlled trials (RCTs) in PTSD from January 1980 to October 2019. Two independent reviewers screened 7,176 records, assessed 2,139 full-text articles, and included 89 studies in 155 publications for this review. Sleep, PTSD, and adverse event outcomes were abstracted and meta-analyses were performed using the Hartung-Knapp-Sidik-Jonkman method for random effects.

Results: Interventions improved sleep outcomes (standardized mean difference [SMD] −0.56; confidence interval [CI] −0.75 to −0.37; 49 RCTs) and PTSD symptoms (SMD −0.48; CI −0.67 to −0.29; 44 RCTs) across studies. Adverse events were not related to interventions overall (RR 1.17; CI 0.91 to 1.49; 15 RCTs). Interventions targeting sleep improved sleep outcomes more than interventions that did not target sleep ($p = .03$). Improvement in PTSD symptoms did not differ between intervention types.

Conclusions: Interventions for patients with PTSD significantly improve sleep outcomes, especially interventions that specifically target sleep. Treatments for adults with PTSD directed toward sleep improvement may benefit patients who suffer from both ailments.

Associations of adverse childhood experiences (ACEs) with sleep duration and quality: The BCOPS study

Charles, L. E., Mnatsakanova, A., Fekedulegn, D., Violanti, J. M., Gu, J. K., & Andrew, M. E. (2022). Associations of adverse childhood experiences (ACEs) with sleep duration and quality: The BCOPS study. *Sleep Medicine, 89,* 166–175. doi:10.1016/j.sleep.2021.12.011

Abstract

Background: Adverse Childhood Experiences (ACEs) are associated with numerous adverse health outcomes in adulthood. Our objective was to investigate associations between ACEs and sleep measures among 206 police officers from the Buffalo Cardio-Metabolic Occupational Police Stress study.

Methods: ACEs (independent variable) was assessed using the ACE questionnaire. Sleep measures were assessed using the Pittsburgh Sleep Quality Index and actigraphy. ANOVA/ANCOVA were used to investigate associations between ACEs and sleep measures.

Results: The mean self-reported sleep duration was significantly lower among participants who reported ≥1 ACEs compared to those who reported no ACEs (6.0 ± 0.11 vs. 6.4 ± 0.14 h; multivariate-adjusted $p = .035$). Sleep efficiency was significantly lower among participants who reported ≥1 ACEs compared to those who reported none (mean = 88.7%, 95% CI = 87.7–89.6 vs. 90.2%, 89.2–91.2; unadjusted $p = .031$) but was slightly attenuated and lost statistical significance after multivariate adjustment (88.8%, 87.8–89.7 vs. 90.1%, 88.9–91.1; $p = .094$). Compared to participants who reported no ACEs, those who reported ≥1 ACEs had a higher mean activity index score (36.9 ± 0.96 vs. 31.2 ± 1.25; multivariate-adjusted $p = .001$); a higher mean wake after sleep onset, WASO (44.3 ± 2.24 vs. 35.3 ± 2.92 min; multivariate-adjusted $p = .019$); and a higher sleep fragmentation index (3.8 ± 1.65 vs. 3.3 ± 1.20, unadjusted $p = .044$; and 3.8 ± 0.13 vs. 3.3 ± 0.18, multivariate-adjusted $p = .062$). Among men (but not women) who reported ≥1 ACEs, self-reported sleep duration was significantly lower (5.9 ± 0.13 vs. 6.4 ± 0.15 h; multivariate-adjusted $p = .025$) and activity index was significantly higher (39.1 ± 1.3 vs. 33.2 ± 1.51; multivariate-adjusted $p = .004$) compared to those who reported no ACEs.

Conclusion: Exposure to ≥1 ACE was associated with worse sleep measures.

Reports of recovered memories in therapy in undergraduate students

Patihis, L., Wood, R. S., Pendergrast, M. H., & Herrera, M. E. (2022). Reports of recovered memories in therapy in undergraduate students. *Psychological Reports, 125*(1), 129–147. doi:10.1177/0033294120971756

Abstract

Psychologists have debated the wisdom of recovering traumatic memories in therapy that were previously unknown to the client, with some concerns over accuracy and memory distortions. The current study surveyed a sample of 576 undergraduates in the south of the United States. Of 188 who reported attending therapy or counseling, 8% reported coming to remember memories of abuse, without any prior recollection of that abuse before therapy. Of those who reported recovered memories, 60% cut off contact with some of their family. Within those who received therapy, those who had a therapist discuss the possibility of repressed memory were 28.6 times more likely to report recovered memories, compared to those who received therapy without such discussion. These findings mirror a previous survey of US adults and suggest attempts to recover repressed memories in therapy may continue in the forthcoming generation of adults.

Detecting presence of PTSD using sentiment analysis from text data

Sawalha, J., Yousefnezhad, M., Shah, Z., Brown, M. R., Greenshaw, A. J., & Greiner, R. (2021). Detecting presence of PTSD using sentiment analysis from text data. *Frontiers in Psychiatry, 12.* doi:10.3389/fpsyt.2021.811392

Abstract

Rates of posttraumatic stress disorder (PTSD) have risen significantly due to the COVID-19 pandemic. Telehealth has emerged as a means to monitor symptoms for such disorders. This is partly due to isolation or inaccessibility of therapeutic intervention caused from the pandemic. Additional screening tools may be needed to augment identification and diagnosis of PTSD through a virtual medium. Sentiment analysis refers to the use of natural language processing (NLP) to extract emotional content from text information. In our study, we train a machine learning (ML) model on text data, which is part of the Audio/Visual Emotion Challenge and Workshop (AVEC-19) corpus, to identify individuals with PTSD using sentiment analysis from semi-structured interviews. Our sample size included 188 individuals without PTSD and 87 with PTSD. The interview was conducted by an artificial character (Ellie) over a video-conference call. Our model was able to achieve a balanced accuracy of 80.4% on a held out dataset used from the AVEC-19 challenge. Additionally, we implemented various partitioning techniques to determine if our model was generalizable enough. This shows that learned models can use sentiment analysis of speech to identify the presence of PTSD, even through a virtual medium. This can serve as an important, accessible and inexpensive tool to detect mental health abnormalities during the COVID-19 pandemic.

Traumatic stress: Effects on the brain

Bremner, J. D. (2022). Traumatic stress: Effects on the brain. *Dialogues in Clinical Neuroscience, 8*(4): 445–461. doi:10.31887/DCNS.2006.8.4/jbremner

Abstract

Brain areas implicated in the stress response include the amygdala, hippocampus, and prefrontal cortex. Traumatic stress can be associated with lasting changes in these brain areas. Traumatic stress is associated with increased cortisol and norepinephrine responses to subsequent stressors. Antidepressants have effects on the hippocampus that counteract the effects of stress. Findings from animal studies have been extended to patients with posttraumatic stress disorder (PTSD) showing smaller hippocampal and anterior cingulate volumes, increased amygdala function, and decreased medial prefrontal/anterior cingulate function. In addition, patients with PTSD show increased cortisol and norepinephrine responses to stress. Treatments that are efficacious for PTSD show a promotion of neurogenesis in animal studies, as well as promotion of memory and increased hippocampal volume in PTSD.

Brain-based biotypes of psychiatric vulnerability in the acute aftermath of trauma

Stevens, J. S., Harnett, N. G., Lebois, L. A., van Rooij, S. J., Ely, T. D., Roeckner, A., . . . Ressler, K. J. (2021). Brain-based biotypes of psychiatric vulnerability in the acute aftermath of trauma. *American Journal of Psychiatry, 178*(11), 1037–1049. doi:10.1176/appi.ajp.2021.20101526

Abstract

Objective: Major negative life events, such as trauma exposure, can play a key role in igniting or exacerbating psychopathology. However, few disorders are diagnosed with respect to precipitating events, and the role of these events in the unfolding of new psychopathology is not well understood. The authors conducted a multisite transdiagnostic longitudinal study of trauma exposure and related mental health outcomes to identify neurobiological predictors of risk, resilience, and different symptom presentations.

Methods: A total of 146 participants (discovery cohort, $N = 69$; internal replication cohort, $N = 77$) were recruited from emergency departments within 72 hours of a trauma and followed for the next six months with a survey, MRI, and physiological assessments.

Results: Task-based functional MRI two weeks after a motor vehicle collision identified four clusters of individuals based on profiles of neural activity reflecting threat reactivity, reward reactivity, and inhibitory engagement. Three clusters were replicated in an independent sample with a variety of trauma types. The clusters showed different longitudinal patterns of posttrauma symptoms.

Conclusions: These findings provide a novel characterization of heterogeneous stress responses shortly after trauma exposure, identifying potential neuroimaging-based biotypes of trauma resilience and psychopathology.

The policing paradox: Police stops predict youth's school disengagement via elevated psychological distress

Del Toro, J., Jackson, D. B., & Wang, M. T. (2022). The policing paradox: Police stops predict youth's school disengagement via elevated psychological distress. *Developmental Psychology.* Advance online publication. doi:10.1037/dev0001361

Abstract

Negative interactions with the legal system can inform adolescents' relationships with schools. The present daily-diary study examined 13,545 daily survey assessments from 387 adolescents (M_{age} = 13–14; 40% male; 32% Black, 50% White, and 18% Other ethnic-racial minority) across 35 days to assess whether police stops predicted adolescents' school disengagement through their psychological distress as a mediator. Results showed that 9% of youth experienced at least one police stop, and 66 stops occurred in total over the 35-day study course. Youth stopped by the police reported greater next-day school disengagement, and youth's psychological distress mediated the link between police stops and school disengagement. Disengagement did not predict youth's next-day police stops. In addition, ethnic-racial minority youth reported more negative police encounters than did White youth, and the effect of a police stop on next-day psychological distress was more negative for Other ethnic-racial minority youth. Implications for reducing police intervention in adolescents' lives are discussed.

www.ingramcontent.com/pod-product-compliance
Lightning Source LLC
LaVergne TN
LVHW082357200926
848481LV00012B/3594